I0027398

COMMODORE MACDONOUGH

Painted by Gilbert Stuart.   Reproduced by permission of Messrs. Rodney and Augustus R. Macdonough.

A List of
PENSIONERS OF THE WAR OF 1812

[Vermont Claimants]

Edited by
Byron N. Clark

Librarian, Vermont Antiquarian Society

With an Appendix containing names of Volunteers for the defence of
Plattsburgh from Vermont towns, a description of the battle from
contemporaneous sources, the official statement of losses, and names
of United States officers and soldiers at Burlington, Vermont,
as shown on army pay and muster rolls recently brought to light.

CLEARFIELD

Originally published
Burlington, Vermont
1904

Reprinted by
Genealogical Publishing Company
Baltimore, Maryland
1969, 1973

Library of Congress Catalog Card Number 73-77981

Reprinted for Clearfield Company by
Genealogical Publishing Company
Baltimore, Maryland
1996, 2012

ISBN 978-0-8063-0074-0

Made in the United States of America

PREFACE

HE Vermont Antiquarian Society has courteously permitted the publication of the interesting record kept by William G. Shaw of Burlington, Vt., during his activity as a pension agent, so far as the notes relate to soldiers in the War of 1812.

This record has particular value as it includes abstracts of the evidence presented by the claimant. There was no Vermont law requiring vital records to be kept by town clerks prior to 1840, hence attempts to learn the families of Vermont soldiers in either the Revolution or the War of 1812 frequently are futile. All who have had occasion to seek genealogical details in Vermont will realize the importance of this pension evidence.

The Volunteers whose names are printed are from the towns of Burlington, Colchester, Huntington, Milton, Underhill, Shelburne, Jericho, and Hinesburgh, and in all, number 189.

The contemporaneous accounts of the battle were copied from the newspaper files in the Fletcher Free Library at Burlington.

By the kindness of Mr. Henry L. Sheldon, we are enabled to add to the appendix, the payrolls of many companies from United States regiments, stationed at Burlington, Vt., during the War of 1812.

The acknowledgements of the editor are due to Messrs. Rodney and Augustus R. Macdonough for the reproduction of the picture of Commodore Macdonough. This is from the portrait painted by Gilbert Stuart, now in the Century Club, New York. The picture of the battle of Plattsburgh is from an old print and is used by permission of Col. C. S. Forbes.

CONTENTS.

NOTES FROM A LIST OF PENSIONERS

OF THE WAR OF 1812 *

AMES, Mehitable,

Aged 80, South Hero, widow of Walter Ames, private in Capt. Moses Bates' Company, Col. William Williams' Regiment, Vermont Militia. He was drafted at Colchester, in the months of June and October, 1813, serving fourteen days. He volunteered in Capt. Bates' Company of Plattsburgh Volunteers, in September, 1814, marched to Plattsburgh, and served there seven days. He was married at Bridgewater, Mass., March 29, 1796, to Mehitable Packard, and died at Salina, Mich., October 23, 1843. Application made July 15, 1856; granted 160 acres of land. Witnesses, Lyman Martin, Benjamin Martin, Justice Henry Robinson.

ANDRES, Samuel,

Aged 60, Chambly, C. E., private in Capt. James Kinney's Company, Col. William Williams' Regiment, Vermont Volunteers. He volunteered at Burlington, September 7, 1814, for the defence of Plattsburgh and was discharged there September 12,

* When no State is given the town is in Vermont.

the discharge being verbal. A muster roll was kept but it was lost or destroyed. Application made January 23, 1858; granted 160 acres of land. Witnesses, Russell S. Taft, E. R. Hard, Justice Torrey E. Wales, John C. Pitcher, Aaron Rowley, M. B. Southwick, and Stephen R. Andres.

ATHERTON, Nancy,

Aged 71, Watertown, N. Y., widow of Chester Atherton, private in Capt. Josiah Barrows' Company of Cavalry, Col. George Tyler's Regiment, Vermont Volunteers. He volunteered at Williston, September 7, 1814, for the defence of Plattsburgh and was discharged there September 12. He was married to Nancy Hall at Castleton, July 17, 1813, by Rev. Elihu Smith, and died at Burlington, February 13, 1842. Application made January 23, 1858. Witnesses, Joseph and Edwina Bostwick, Justice William Weston, Childs Day, Jesse J. Starr, and Paul T. Sweet, of Burlington, James M. Clark and Alonzo M. Rogers, of Watertown, N. Y.

Nancy Hall Atherton was married to Timothy Hungerford at Rutland, N. Y., July 3, 1844, by Rev. Mr. Spaulding, and Hungerford died at Watertown, N. Y., November 22, 1857. No other record of either marriage in existence.

BARTLETT, Eber,

Aged 73, Hadley, N. Y., private in Capts. Reed and Allen's Company, Vermont Volunteer Militia. He volunteered at Jericho, in September, 1814, for the defence of Plattsburgh, served seven days, was discharged at Burlington, September 13, 1814, having taken part in the battle of September 11. Application made September 17, 1856; granted 160 acres of land. Witnesses, George Kenyon, Jonathan Crannell, Justice Reuben Wills, of Warren Co., N. Y., Luther Prouty, Sylvanus Blodgett, Justice Erastus Field.

BATES, Huldah,
Aged 66, New Haven, widow of Levi Bates, private in Capt. James Talcott's Company, Vermont Militia. He volunteered at Williston, September 9, 1814, for the defence of Plattsburgh, served four days, and was discharged there, September 12, 1814, having taken part in the battle of September 11. He was married to Huldah Graves at Richmond, September 3, 1810, by Abel Cooper, J. P., and died there March 21, 1827. No public or private record of the marriage in existence till now. Raised large family of children. Application made August 21, 1856; granted 160 acres of land. Witnesses, Levi Rockwood and Watson C. Washburn, of New Haven, Justice Jonathan Hough, James Talcott, Elisha Wright, Justice William Weston.

BENEDICT, George W.,
Aged 60, Burlington, private in Capt. Jacob Howell's Company, Col. Farrington's Regiment, New York Militia. He was drafted at Franklin, N. Y., September 8, 1814, and discharged at New York City, October 22, 1814. Application made May 28, 1856; granted 160 acres of land. Witnesses, Miles A. Evarts, George L. Reynolds, Justice Jno. B. Hollenbeck.

BENHAM, John,

Aged 69, Jericho, teamster in United States service. He volunteered at Jericho, March 21, 1813, serving thirteen days. He was engaged in transporting the troops of General Chandler's brigade from Burlington to Canton, N. Y., being paid for such service $39.00, in September, 1813, by George Wadsworth, a United States paymaster. He was drafted as a private, in October, 1813, in Capt. Oliver Lowrey's Company, Third Regiment of the Vermont Militia, under Col. George Tyler, and was discharged at Burlington, October 17, 1813. He was a private in Capt. Myron Reed's Company, Col. George Tyler's Regiment, Vermont Volunteers, having volunteered at Jericho, about September 7, 1814, for the defence of Plattsburgh. He was discharged at Burlington, September 13, 1814, having been present at the battle of Plattsburgh, September 11. Application made May 28, 1856; granted 160 acres of land. Witnesses, Joel Rood and Luther Prouty, of Jericho, Justice David Fish, Harvey Field, Edy Humphrey.

BLISS, Arrabert F.,

Aged 21, Green Lake, Wis., son of Julius Bliss, private in company commanded by Capt. Myron Reed and Capt. Peter L. Allen, Col. George Tyler's Regiment, Vermont Militia. He volunteered at Jericho, September 7, 1814, for the defence of Plattsburgh, and was discharged at Burlington, September 13. He died at Jericho, September 7, 1845, leaving a widow, Mary Bliss, who was married to Pelatiah Bliss in the summer of 1849. Application made March 19, 1858. Witnesses, Philo F. and Delia Drury and Justice D. H. Seaver.

BROWN, Polly,

Aged 71, Jericho, widow of Joseph Brown, teamster, who was drafted at Plattsburgh, March 12, 1813, being pressed into service while absent from home with his team. He was employed to transport military stores from Plattsburgh to Sackett's Harbor, N. Y., being absent twenty-two days, being paid in part at the latter place by Paymaster Wolsey, and at Burlington by George Wadsworth. He was married to Polly Cady at Jericho, July 10, 1808, by ――― Theall, J. P.; had children, Rufus, Mary, and David. Application made July 30, 1856. Witnesses, Rufus Brown, Mary Brown, and Justice William Weston.

BROWNELL, Thomas,

Aged 68, Colchester. He volunteered at Colchester, September 6, 1814, for the defence of Plattsburgh, serving in the commissary department, commanded by John Waford. He was discharged at Plattsburgh, September 12. He crossed Lake Champlain on September 7, in a skiff with four others and landed on Crab Island. On the day of the battle of Plattsburgh he was engaged in guarding provisions in a scow on the lake. Application made September 29, 1856. Witnesses, Joshua S. Sackett, Gay H. Narramore, Justice William M. Peck, Elijah W. Wood, of Huberton, N. Y., and Amos Boardman, of Wheaton, Illinois.

CHURCHILL, Gilbert,

Genessee, N. Y., private in Capt. Moses Bates' Company, Col. George Tyler's Regiment, Vermont Militia. He was drafted at Colchester, June 10, 1813, and served about five days, and again in the same company in October, serving fourteen days, for three or four days acting as a teamster under Quartermaster Wadsworth, in transporting stores from Burlington to Plattsburgh. Application made June 12, 1856.

EVEREST, Harry,

Aged 60, Milton, private in Capt. William Picket's Company, Vermont Volunteer Militia. He volunteered at Addison, September 6, 1814, for the defence of Plattsburgh and served seven days, being discharged there September 12, having taken an active part in the defence. The discharge of his company was verbal, and the rolls were lost. Application made September 26, 1856. Witnesses, Ira W. Everest, of Addison, Charles M. Gay, of Milwaukee, Wis., Justice William Weston, Daniel G. Wilkins, of Addison, Justice George Willmarth.

FIELD, Harvey,

Aged 66, Jericho, private in company commanded by Capt. Myron Reed and Lieut. Peter L. Allen in Col. George Tyler's Regiment, Vermont Volunteers. He volunteered at Jericho, September 7, 1814, for the defence of Plattsburgh, served seven days, and was discharged at Burlington, September 13. Application made May 28, 1856; granted 160 acres of land. Witnesses, Luther Prouty, Edy Humphrey, of Jericho, Justice David Fish, John Benham, Jonas Marsh, of Jericho, Justice Hosea Spaulding.

FISHER, Olive,

Aged 60, Bolton, widow of John L. Fisher, private in Capt. Hale's Company, Eleventh Regiment, United States Volunteers. He enlisted at Barre, in June, 1812, served for five years, and was discharged at New York, in June, 1817. He was married at Bolton, March 24, 1820, to Olive Colbarth, by John Pinneo, J. P., and died in the same town, June 14, 1854. Application made May 24, 1856, but rejected because of desertion. Witnesses, John B. Sabens, of Bolton, Luther Prouty, of Jericho, Justice Erastus Field.

FULLER, David,

Aged 63, Nepenskua, Wis., private in Capt. Ithiel Stone's Company, Vermont Militia. He volunteered at Monkton, in September, 1814, for the defence of Plattsburgh, in which he took an active part, and was discharged at Burlington, September 15, 1814. Application made May 16, 1856; granted 160 acres of land. Witnesses, James Wheeler and Samuel Clough, of Nepenskua, Wis., Justice William Elliott, Charles A. Weisbrod, County Clerk of Winnebago County, Wis. Jno. Hollenbeck and Levi Cogswell testify that they were in the same company, etc.

GOODWIN, Aaron,

Aged 62, Hermon, N. Y., private in Capt. Moses Jewett's Company, Vermont Militia. He was drafted at Burlington, June 10, 1813, served four days, and was again drafted, October 3,

1813, serving twelve days. Application made March 12, 1856.
Witnesses, William Freeman, Elisha Burnham, Justice William
Tanner. Case rejected because of wrong evidence.

HALL, Charlotte,

Aged 55, Milton, widow of Alpheus Hall, private in Capt.
Jonathan Prentiss' Company, Col. Jacob Davis' Regiment, Vermont Militia. They were married at South Hero, October 6,
1820, by Rev. Asa Lyon. Hall died at Milton, October 18,
1855. Application made July 14, 1856. Witnesses, D.
French, William H. French, Justice Torrey E. Wales, Clarissa
Hall, and Caroline H. Smith.

HOWE, Brigham,

Aged 76, Potsdam, N. Y., private in company commanded
by Capt. Myron Reed and Lieut. Peter L. Allen, in Col.
George Tyler's Regiment, Vermont Militia. He volunteered at
Jericho, September 7, 1814, and was discharged at Burlington,
September 13, having taken part in the defence of Plattsburgh.
Application made July 21, 1856; granted 160 acres of land.
Witnesses, Truman Lillie and Charley Bailey, of Potsdam, N. Y.,
Justice Amos Blood, Luther Prouty, and Sylvanus Blodgett.

HUMPHREY, Edy,

Aged 66, Jericho, private in company commanded by Capt.
Myron Reed and Lieut. Peter L. Allen, Col. George Tyler's
Regiment, Vermont Militia. He volunteered at Jericho, Septem-

ber 7, 1814, and was discharged at Burlington, September 13, after having been present at the battle of Plattsburgh. Application made May 28, 1856; granted 160 acres of land.

HURLBUT, Philena,

Aged 65, Moriah, N. Y., widow of Chauncey Hurlbut, private in Capt. Barnes' Company, Col. William Williams' Regiment, Vermont Militia. He was drafted at St. Albans, in June or July, 1812, and was discharged at Swanton, in December, 1812. He volunteered at Colchester for the defence of Plattsburgh and served under Capt. Moses Bates in Col. George Tyler's Regiment, Vermont Militia. He was married to Philena Severance at Colchester, July 5, 1814, by William Hine, J. P., and died at Moriah, N. Y., March 3, 1841. Application made August 25, 1856; granted 160 acres of land. Witnesses, John and George Severance, of Colchester, Justice George P. Mayo, George Sherman, and E. S. Edgerton, of Moriah, N. Y.

HUTCHINS, Betsey,

Aged 84, Jericho, widow of Eleazer Hutchins, surgeon in Col. George Tyler's Regiment, Vermont Militia. He was drafted at Jericho, October 1, 1813, and discharged at Burlington, October 17. He volunteered at Jericho, September 7, 1814, for the defence of Plattsburgh, and was discharged at Burlington, September 18. He was married to Betsey Hollenbeck at Jericho, in August, 1790, by Samuel Darrow, J. P., and died February 22, 1833. Application made May 28, 1856; granted

160 acres of land. Witnesses, David and Betsey L. Fish, of Jericho, Luther Prouty, John Benham, Harvey Field, and Justice Hosea Spaulding.

HUTCHINS, Elijah S.,

Aged 59, Milwaukee, Wis., private in company commanded by Capt. Myron Reed and Lieut. Peter L. Allen, in Col. George Tyler's Regiment, Vermont Militia. He volunteered at Jericho, September 7, 1814, for the defence of Plattsburgh. During the day he was made assistant to his father, Eleazer, who was surgeon of the regiment, and helped care for the wounded during the battle and for a few days after. He was discharged at Plattsburgh, September 14. Application made October 7, 1856. Witnesses, William E. Webster and Charles McDonald, of Milwaukee, Wis., Justice William Holland, William Rouse, and Sylvanus Blodgett.

LANDON, Julius C.,

Aged 70, Sharon Springs, N. Y., fifer in Capt. James Kinney's Company, Col. William Williams' Regiment, Vermont Militia. He volunteered at Shelburne, September 7, 1814, marched to Burlington, crossed Lake Champlain to Plattsburgh. There the company was mustered into service, served during the battle, and was discharged, September 12. The pay rolls were lost and he never received a written discharge. Application made June 12, 1857. Witnesses, Marshall N. DeMoyelles, Nathan W. Stratton, Justice William E. Sprong, John F. Shafer, Clerk of

Schoharie County, Garrad Burritt, Levi Comstock, Justice William Weston, and Bostwick Tousley, who was in the same company, near Landon.

LYMAN, Stephen,

Aged 71, Jericho, private in company commanded by Capt. Myron Reed and Lieut. Peter L. Allen, Col. George Tyler's Regiment, Vermont Militia. He volunteered at Jericho, September 7, 1814, for the defence of Plattsburgh, and was discharged at Burlington, September 13, after active service at the battle of September 11. Application made July 30, 1856; granted 160 acres of land.

MARSH, Jonas,

Aged 72, Jericho, private in company commanded by Capt. Myron Reed and Lieut. Peter L. Allen, Col. George Tyler's Regiment, Vermont Militia. He volunteered at Jericho, September 7, 1814, for the defence of Plattsburgh, and was discharged at Burlington, September 13, after having taken part in the battle. Application made May 28, 1856. Witnesses, Luther Prouty and Joel Reed, of Jericho, Justice David Fish, Harvey Field, John Benham, and Justice Hosea Spaulding.

MATTHEWS, Jeremiah,

Aged 63, Williston, sergeant in Capt. James Talcott's Company, Vermont Militia. He volunteered at Williston, September 9,

1814, for the defence of Plattsburgh, crossed Lake Champlain, September 10; during the battle of September 11 he helped to guard the ammunition wagons ; was discharged at Plattsburgh, September 12. He formerly was in the service at Burlington, in 1813, in Capt. Morton's Company, Vermont Militia. Application made September 17, 1856; granted 160 acres of land. Witnesses, Mackson Burdick, of Westford, Timothy Peters, of Shelburne, Justice William Weston, James Talcott and Elisha Wright, of Williston, Justice John Snyder.

MERRILL, Hannah,

Aged 69, Colchester, widow of Arad Merrill, lieutenant in company commanded by Capt. James Taylor or Capt. Joseph Beeman, Col. Dixon's Regiment, Vermont Militia. He volunteered at Westford, September 8, 1814, for the defence of Plattsburgh, and was discharged there September 13. He was married to Hannah Bean at New Grantham, N. H., February 24, 1805, by Rev. Simeon Short and died at Colchester, January 22, 1849. Application made March 31, 1857. Witnesses, Andrew J. Merrill, Charles H. Storrs, Justice William W. Peck, Bartholomew F. Taylor, of Essex, and Henry Bowman, of Franklin.

MURRAY, Mary,

Aged 62, Williston, widow of Robert Murray, private in Capt. Hezekiah Barnes' Company, Col. William Williams' Regiment, Vermont Detached Militia. He was drafted at Burlington, July 1, 1812, and was discharged at Swanton, December 1,

1812. He was married to Mary Sherman at Waterbury, in September, 1819, by Dan Carpenter, J. P., and died at Williston, in July, 1831. Application made March 17, 1856; granted 160 acres of land. Witnesses, Aurelia Murray, Curtis Murray, and Justice William Weston.

NICHOLS, Rebecca,

Aged 62, Marcellus, N. Y., widow of Jesse Nichols, private in Capt. Warren Ellis' Company, Col. Parley Davis' Regiment, Vermont Volunteers. He volunteered at Barre, September 7, 1814, for the defence of Plattsburgh, and was discharged there, September 14. He was married to Rebecca Herring at Barre, May 8, 1815, by Warren Ellis, Esq., and died at Burlington, April 11, 1839. Application made November 29, 1853; granted 160 acres of land. Witnesses, Truman A. Eggleston and Absalom Herring, of Marcellus, N. Y., Justice Sidney H. Cook, and Samuel Nichols.

ORBIN, Henry,

Aged 62, Burlington, private and corporal in Capt. Rogers' Company, Twenty-ninth Regiment, Maryland Militia. He was drafted at Baltimore, Md., in April, May, or June, 1814, and was discharged there in October, November, or December of the same year. Application made May 6, 1856; case suspended for lack of evidence. Witnesses, Samuel Huntington and Martha Miller, of Burlington, and William G. Shaw.

PARSONS, Sylvanus,

Aged 57, Jericho, private in company commanded by Capt. Peter L. Allen, Col. George Tyler's Regiment, Vermont Militia. He volunteered at Jericho, September 7, 1814, and was discharged at Burlington, September 13, after service in defence of Plattsburgh. "Said company volunteered under Capt. Myron Reed, who commanded the Infantry Company at Jericho aforesaid, at the time. But Capt. Reed from ill health was unable to take the command at Plattsburgh, and Capt. Peter L. Allen was appointed in his stead." Application made July 26, 1856; granted 160 acres of land. Witnesses, Luther Prouty, Samuel Quincy, Justice Erastus Field, and Nathan Smith.

PROUTY, Hepzibah,

Aged 66, Jericho, widow of Luther Prouty, sergeant in company commanded by Capt. Myron Reed and Lieut. Peter L. Allen, Col. George Tyler's Regiment, Vermont Militia. He volunteered at Jericho, September 7, 1814, for the defence of Plattsburgh, served during the battle, and was discharged at Burlington, September 13. He was married to Hepzibah Howe at Jericho, October 28, 1815, by Rev. Ephraim Butler and died at Richmond, February 12, 1857. Application made July 13, 1857; granted 160 acres of land. Witnesses, Harvey Field, Stephen Lyman, Oliver Lowrey, David Fish, and Justice Erastus Field.

PROUTY, Luther,

Aged 68, Jericho, sergeant in company commanded by Capt. Myron Reed and Lieut. Peter L. Allen, Col. George Tyler's

Regiment, Vermont Volunteers. He volunteered at Jericho, September 7, 1814, and was discharged at Burlington, September 13, after serving in the defence of Plattsburgh. Application made May 28, 1856; case discontinued because of death of Prouty. Witnesses, Harvey Field and Edy Humphrey, of Jericho, Justice Erastus Field, Jonas Marsh, and Justice Hosea Spaulding.

QUINCY, Samuel,
Aged 68, Underhill, sergeant in Capt. Peter L. Allen's Company, Col. George Tyler's Regiment, Vermont Militia. He volunteered at Jericho, September 7, 1814, and was discharged at Burlington, September 13, after serving in the defence of Plattsburgh. Application made July 30, 1856. Witnesses, Luther Prouty, Sylvanus M. Parsons, Justice William Weston, and Justice Erastus Field.

REED, Huldah,
Aged 74, Jericho, widow of Thomas Reed, private in company commanded by Capt. Myron Reed and Lieut. Peter L. Allen, Col. George Tyler's Regiment, Vermont Militia. He volunteered at Jericho, September 7, 1814, and was discharged at Burlington, September 13, after serving in the defence of Plattsburgh. He was married to Huldah Rockwell at Jericho, August 1, 1813, by Rev. Ephraim Butler and died at Burlington, November 23, 1836. Application made July 30, 1856; granted 160 acres of land. Witnesses, Luther Prouty, Daniel L. Hale, Justice William Weston, Samuel Quincy, and Hepzibah Prouty.

Rood, Silas S.,

Aged 66, Sugar Creek, Wis., private in Capt. Beeman's Company, Vermont Volunteers.   He volunteered at Milton, September 7, 1814, for the defence of Plattsburgh and was discharged there, September 13.   Application made September 13, 1856.   Witnesses, James M. Lucton, Alonzo Rublee, Justice Samuel A. Tibbetts, Timothy Percival, of Jericho, and Bartholomew F. Taylor, of Essex.

Rowley, Aaron,

Aged 69, Shelburne, sergeant in the company commanded by Capt. James Kinney, under Major Judson, Col. William Williams' Regiment, Vermont Militia.   He volunteered at Shelburne, September 7, 1814, going directly to Plattsburgh, where, on the day of the battle, his company was stationed near a bridge over the Saranac River to prevent the British troops from crossing; this bridge they guarded until the British retreated at night. Application made May 28, 1856; granted 160 acres of land. Witnesses, Betsey T. W. Rowley and Frances Witters, of Shelburne, Justice William Weston, Garrad Burritt, and Levi Comstock, of Shelburne.

Seely, Gilmore,

Aged 65, Jericho, private in Capt. Danforth's Company, Thirtieth Regiment, United States Infantry.   He enlisted at Middlebury in the spring of 1813, and was discharged at Burlington, the fall of the same year, because of poor health, after having spent much time in the United States hospital there.   Application made May 24, 1856. Witnesses, Henry E. Hoskins, of Jericho, N. B. Proctor, of Burlington, and Justice William Weston.

SIPLE, Christiana,

Aged 88, Charlotte, widow of Michael Siple, teamster in the United States service. He served in the transportation of troops and provisions from Burlington to Sackett's Harbor, N. Y., from the middle of March to April 7, 1813, having been pressed into service at Charlotte. He was discharged at Sackett's Harbor and was paid by Joseph Keeler, who was in the United States service, either as a quartermaster or an assistant. He was married to Christiana Harrington at Nine Partners, N. Y., July 2, 1786, by Myers Place, J. P., and died at Ferrisburgh, March 28, 1846. Application made February 27, 1856; granted 160 acres of land. Witnesses, S. H. Tupper and James Jones, of Charlotte, Justice A. L. Beach, Levi Cogswell, and Daniel Ball, of Charlotte, and Justice S. M. Parsons.

SPAULDING, Andrew,

Aged 68, Bangor, N. Y., private in Capt. James Talcott's Company, Vermont Militia. He volunteered at Williston, September 9, 1814, for the defence of Plattsburgh, where he was discharged, September 12. Application made September 1, 1856; granted 160 acres of land. Witnesses, Lucius Bigelow, James Talcott, Justice William Weston, Elisha Wright, and Justice John Snyder.

SPEAR, Barnabas,

Aged 72, Colchester, private in Capt. Henry Mayo's Company,

Col. William Williams' Regiment, Vermont Militia. He volunteered at Burlington, September 7, 1814, for the defence of Plattsburgh and was discharged there, September 12. No pay roll of the company exists and the company was never paid; the rolls were lost or destroyed. Application made June 9, 1857; granted 160 acres of land. Witnesses, Capt. Henry Mayo, James Morse, E. W. Peck, and Sayles Nichols.

TALCOTT, James,

Aged 65, Williston, captain in Vermont Militia. He volunteered at Williston, September 9, 1814, for the defence of Plattsburgh and was mustered out there, September 12. "Said company organized at Burlington, Vt., September 9, 1814. On the morning of the 10th I drew arms from Arthur Bostwick, quartermaster at said Burlington; crossed Lake Champlain the same day; arrived at Plattsburgh the next morning; was mustered into service; drew rations and ammunitions; and served with my Company during the day of the Battle, guarding ammunition wagons, and the day after the Battle our Company having been honorably discharged verbally from further service said Company returned home. No roll of this Company has been preserved to my knowledge, and I believe that none exists." Application made June 9, 1856; granted 160 acres of land. Witnesses, Elisha Wright, John Munson, and Justice Jno. B. Hollenbeck

THAYER, Ruth,

Aged 79, Shelburne, widow of Eli Thayer, private in Capt.

James Kinney's Company, Maj. Judson's Regiment, Vermont Militia. He volunteered at Shelburne, September 7, 1814, for the defence of Plattsburgh, in a company from Shelburne, took part in the battle, and was discharged there, September 13. He was married to Ruth Messenger at Shelburne, December 3, 1795, by Rev. Mr. Gillett, and died there October 26, 1838. Application made July 20, 1857. Witnesses, Lyman and Laura Thayer, Levi Comstock, and Garrad Burritt.

WALBRIDGE, Betsey,

Aged 62, Stanbridge, C. E., widow of Solomon Walbridge, private in Capt. Wooster's Company, Vermont Militia. He volunteered at St. Albans, September 6, 1814, for the defence of Plattsburgh, and was discharged there, September 12. He was married to Betsey McKinster at Cambridge, September 29, 1818, and died at Stanbridge, March 20, 1854. Application made August 31, 1857. Witnesses, Alexander S. Walbridge and Charles Phelps, of Stanbridge, M. M. Walbridge, Jonathan W. Blaisdell, of St. Albans, and Hiram Hopkins, of Cambridge.

WELLS, Joseph,

Aged 79, Fletcher, private in Capt. James English's Company, Col. Parley Davis' Regiment, Vermont Militia. He volunteered at Marshfield, September 9, 1814. The company marched to Burlington, where it was organized, the men choosing their own officers. Capt. English then reported his company of volunteers for the defence of Plattsburgh to Col. Fassett, a United States officer then in command at Burlington, under whose command the company drew arms, ammunition, and provisions from the military stores there. Wells was put in charge of the rations of the company, issuing them to the soldiers. On the morning of September 11 they embarked from Burlington on a government sloop for Plattsburgh, but because of lack of wind they did not arrive on the New York shore until late in the afternoon. They camped that night where they landed, about five miles south of Plattsburgh, and the next morning marched to the town where they remained organized until the following Wednesday when, the British having retreated to Canada, they went to Burlington, returning the United States arms and being discharged September 15. Application made July 17, 1856; granted 160 acres of land. Witnesses, Henry Weed, Homer S. Chandler, and Justice William Weston.

WILLIS, Hannah,

Aged 70, Burlington, widow of Stoughton Willis, teamster in the War of 1812. He was married to Hannah Woodruff, at Westford, December 25, 1805, by Ezra Slater, J. P., and died at Chateaugay, N. Y., January 2, 1842, and was buried at Keeseville. Application made July 22, 1857; granted 160 acres of land. Witnesses, Susannah and Charles P. Higbee.

WRIGHT, Brigham C.,

Aged 62, Milton, sergeant in Capt. James Talcott's Company, Vermont Militia. He volunteered at Williston, September 9,

1814, for the defence of Plattsburgh, where he was discharged September 12.   On the morning of the day of the battle the company was mustered into service, drew rations and ammunition from the military stores, and was then placed to guard the ammunition wagons against the British troops from whom an attack was expected.   The attack was made and the company retreated to a more secure position, being under the command of United States officers.   Application made July 16, 1856; granted 160 acres of land.   Witnesses, William H. French, George A. French, and Justice David French.

WRIGHT, Elisha,
Aged 62, Williston, private in Capt. James Talcott's Company, Vermont Militia.   He volunteered at Williston, September 9, 1814, for the defence of Plattsburgh, going there on the 10th. On the day of the battle the company was in charge of the ammunition wagons, was attacked by a large force of the British, and was compelled to retreat, being under command of the United States officers.   He was discharged at Plattsburgh, September 12.   Application made July 16, 1856; granted 160 acres of land.   Witnesses, James Talcott, John Munson, and Justice Jno. Hollenbeck.

OTHER RECORDS

COATS, Asahel,

Aged 52, Russelltown, C. E., private in company commanded by Lieut. Warner and Capt. E. M. Kirby, First Regiment, United States Artillery, commanded by Col. Pierce in the Florida War. He enlisted at Utica, N. Y., under Lieut. H. Day, June 24, 1836, for three years. He was in actual service in the first war in the territory of Florida, for five months and fourteen days, and was discharged at Rouse's Point, N. Y., April 24, 1839. Granted 160 acres of land. Witnesses, Fisher Ames, William Racecot, of Russelltown, C. E.

CURTIS, Lucinda,

Aged 77, Lewis, N. Y., widow of Zachariah Curtis, private in the Revolutionary War, serving six years and nine months. He was married to Lucinda Newton at Moretown, August 17, 1833, by Cephas Carpenter and died at Charlotte, August 23, 1839. Application made October 19, 1857. Witnesses, Theodore Isham, of Essex, N. Y., and Jonathan Wrisley, of Lewis, N. Y.

VOLUNTEERS FOR PLATTSBURGH

VOLUNTEERS FOR PLATTSBURGH.

COLCHESTER, VT.

Captain Moses Bates,
Lieutenant William Hyde,
Ensign Joseph Chandler,
Sergeant William Ellis,
Sergeant Jacob Bates,
Nathan Bryan,
Abner Mack,
George Woolcott,
David Bean,
Ebenezer Johnson,
Cyrus Farrand,
Noah Woolcott,
Ebenezer Allen,
Isaac Thompson,
Barney Fisher,
Simeon Fisher,
Chauncey Hurlburt,
Paul Clapp,
Walter Ames,
Elisha Boardman,
Melzer Packard,
Cyrus Ames,
David Whitney,
William Persons,

Joseph Fleming,
Joel Butler,
Joseph Plan (or Plue),
John Plan (or Plue), Jr.,
Reuben Jones,
Heman Washburn,
Timothy Gale,
Samuel Richardson,
Elnathan Ellis,
Billy Ames,
Jonathan Boardman,
Lyman Ellis,
Thomas Brownell.

HUNTINGTON, VT.

Captain Artemus Farr,
Ensign James Ambler,
Corporal Frederick Ambler,
Corporal Daniel Scofield,
John F. Firman,
John Brewster,
Jacob Pierce,
David Caswell,
Asa Wells,
Giles Rood,
Nathan Holley,
Jacob Sherman,
Peter Shattuck,
Comfort Brewster,

James Hoskins,
John Snyder,
David Scofield,
Orin Byington,
Samuel Bunker,
John Buell,
Noah Johnson,
Levi Shattuck,
Asa Gillett,
James H. Nichols,
John Fitch.

JERICHO, VT.

Jonas Marsh,
John Benham,
John Thompson,
William Rouse,
Luther Prouty,
Stephen Lyman,
Sylvanus Blodgett,
Harvey Field,
William Smith,
Harry M. Wilder,
Edy Humphrey,
Salmon Fay,
Philander Benham,
John Porter,
John Porter, Jr.,
Azariah Rouse,

Zebedee Packard,
Nathan Smith,
John Downing,
Surgeon Eleazer Hutchins,
Eber Bartlett,
Charles How,
Brigham How,
Warren Ford,
Silas S. Rood,
Myron Chapin,
William P. Richardson,
William Rood,
James Rood,
Stephen Lane,
Abijah Whitton,
Nathan Smith,
Julius Bliss,
Thomas Reed,
Oliver Wilder,
Jedediah Lane,
Henry Howe,
Oliver Rouse,
Lewis Johnson,
James Thompson,
William Brown,
Heman N. Hurlburt,
Sergeant Nathan Scranton

MILTON, VT.

Asa C. Pettee.

UNDERHILL, VT.

Captain Elijah Burge,
Samuel Quincy,
Peter Martin,
Eli Woodruff,
Jeremiah Matthews,
Benjamin Parker,
Wright Hurlburt,
Josiah Mead,
Martin Mead,
John Atchinson,
Abraham Story,
Eli Whitten,
Ralph Woodworth,
Truman Sheldon.

SHELBURNE, VT.

Chester Blinn,
Alvah Tyler,
Aaron Rowley,
Garrad Burritt,
Levi Comstock,
Robert Averill,
Hyman Holabird,
Charles Spear,
Simon Judson,
William Blin,
Reuben Burritt,
Timothy Holabird,

Daniel Barron,
John Barron,
Burgess Hall,
Abijah Allen,
Eli Thayer,
Samuel Peters,
Salmon H. Keeler,
Captain D. Hough,
John Hosford,
Samuel B. Kennedy,
Ephraim Webster,
John Pinneo,
Noah Wilcox.

BURLINGTON, VT.

Captain Henry Mayo,
Sergeant George Lewis,
Corporal Francis Faxon,
James Morse,
Simon Willard,
Levi Willard,
Alphonso Collins,
William Blush,
David Mayo,
Dubartis Willard,
Holden Farnsworth,
Eli Kimball,
Henry Blush,
Jacob Underhill,

Thomas Eddy,
John Lathrop,
Philander Kellogg,
——— Kellogg,
Moses Kendall,
——— Weaver,
Jacob Darling,
Ezra Wardwrought,
——— Sanderson.

HUNTINGTON AND HINESBURGH COMPANY OF HORSE.

Captain Josiah N. Barrows,
Jeremiah Abby,
John Ambler,
Samuel Brewster,
Charles Brewster,
Solomon Baker,
Jabez Fargo,
Harry Hurlburt,
Chester Atherton,
Sherman Beach,
Robert Beach,
Asahel Stacy,
Childs Day,
Amara W. Clark,
Silas McLellan,
Allen Freeman,
John Fay,
William White,
Zadock Blin.

ROLL OF VERMONT VOLUNTEERS, MADE AT BURLINGTON, VT., SEPT. 9, 1814.

Othanil Jewett, captain,
Ephraim Munson, first lieutenant,
James Wilcox, second lieutenant,
Jeremy Bradley, ensign,
Roger Noble, sergeant,
Luther Hunt, sergeant,
John A. Sumner, sergeant,
Daniel Twitchell, sergeant,
William Sampson, Jr., corporal,
Thomas Brintnell, Jr., corporal,
Eli Sprague, corporal,
Christopher Beebe, corporal,
William Richardson, corporal,
Daniel Cole,
Samuel Sumner,
Myron Chittenden,
Eben Chittenden,
Seth Griswold,
Elisha Pettibone,
Manford Pier, deserter,
Russell Eastman, deserter,
Abel P. Wightman,
Nathan Griffeths,
Enoch Sprague,
George Harrington,
Thomas Clark,
Eliphalet Tousley,
John Rider,

Lyardus Tousley,
Everts Griswold,
Simeon Jennings,
William Bullard,
Amos P. Nash,
Amos Field,
Robert Holley,
Isaac Buttolph,
Alvin J. Wadkins,
Thomas Briggs,
Israel Barker,
William L. Clark,
Abel Mead,
Nathan Sprague,
Andalotia Pier,
Joshua Hildreth,
Thomas Perkins,
Alexander Carter,
Samuel Newbury,
Amanza Ladd,
Russell Eastman,
Harry Kilbourn,
William Manross,
James Fuller,
Harvey Chilson,
Stephen Ballom,
David Munson,
Almon Beeman,
Mr. Holbrook,
Moses F. Wheeler,
Amos Bird,

Rufus Barnard,
Ezekiel Lawrence,
Stephen Lee,
Sewell Merritt, deserter,
Alexander Dudley, deserter,
John Myres,
Samuel Stewart,
Israel West, Jr.,
John Wilkinson,
Hiram Chilson.

"Said copy above written has been this 14th day of May,
A. D. 1855, read over and compared by me, the said Isaac
Buttolph, and is a true copy of the original roll of said Capt.
Jewett's company."

[Signed]   Isaac Buttolph,
James Wilcox.

George Fisher,
Ira Willmarth, lieutenant,
William Whitford, ensign,
Freedom Jackson, orderly sergeant,
Samuel Day, orderly sergeant,
Amos Willmarth, sergeant,
Jesse Smith, assistant orderly sergeant,
Lyman Clark, corporal,
Ephraim Jackson, corporal,
George Willmarth, corporal,
Wickliff G. Post, corporal,
Benjamin Billart, sergeant,
Jacob Post, sergeant,

David H. Post,
Rufus Smith,
Ansel Hawks,
James Curtis,
Amos Smith,
Henry Smith,
Daniel Smith,
Henry Fisher,
Jeremiah Day,
Gideon Carpenter,
Russell Smith,
Jonathan Pratt,
James Patterson,
Abel Willmarth,
Isaac Case,
Samuel Pond,
Asa Willmarth,
John Looker,
Daniel G. Wilkins,
Sylvester Pond,
John Heaton,
Ashel Clark,
Martin Luther,
William Jackson,
Chester Elmore,
Josiah Coalridge,
Joshua Whitney,
Calvin Skinner,
Thurstin Bullard,
Charles Spencer, musician,
Joseph Callam, musician,

Risalaid Day, musician,
James Daily,
Caleb Post,
John Post,
David Fairchild,
John Snell,
Hezekiah Jackson,
Samuel Brown, second.

" The following names are those that went to Plattsburgh from the West company of Addison, Vt., commanded by Capt. Picket."

William Picket, captain,
William Vanwert,
Ebenezer Hayward,
Archibald Bloomfield,
Ira Strong,
John Herriman,
Ira W. Everts,
Martin Baldwin,
Allen Smith,
Matthew Chambers,
John Hurd,
John Benedict,
Hiram Everst.

"A great part of the above named persons I distinctly recollect being at the battle of Plattsburgh, A. D. 1814, and should be willing to testify to this fact."

[Signed]   George Willmarth.

THE BATTLE OF PLATTSBURGH.

From an old print. Reproduced by permission of Col. C. S. Forbes, Editor of " The Vermonter."

APPENDIX

ACCOUNTS OF THE BATTLE OF PLATTS-BURGH, SEPTEMBER 11, 1814

T HE following account is taken from an "extra" of the "Northern Sentinel," published at Burlington, Vt., on Tuesday, September 13, 1814.

"GLORIOUS INTELLIGENCE."

" The anxiety of the public to learn the particulars of the late splendid victory over the British squadron on this Lake, has induced us to publish the following, which are all that have come to our knowledge.

" On Sunday, the ever memorable 11th of September, the enemy's squadron was discovered about eight o'clock, A. M., standing up the lake with a favorable breeze, under a press of sail. Every preparation was made by our gallant Commodore to give them a warm and cordial reception; with his squadron at anchor he awaited their approach. The enemy soon made their appearance off Cumberland Head and bore down for our squadron—the enemy's two largest vessels taking a position to attack the Saratoga, our flag ship. The first broadside from her killed the British Commodore (Downie) and her fire continued so spirited and well directed that the enemy's flag ship, the Confiance, soon after struck. At this time the whole broadside guns of the Saratoga next to the enemy were completely unmanageable. The enemy's brig continued her fire.

Our Commodore slipped his cable and wore round; two broadsides compelled the brig to follow the example of the Confiance. In the meantime the Preble compelled one of the enemy's sloops to strike. The other grounded on Hospital Island just before the battle ended, and was taken possession of by some of our Gallies. The enemy's Gallies, except two which were sunk, with the assistance of their oars effected their escape. The slaughter on board the British fleet was immense. The Confiance alone had 110 killed and wounded. Our loss is severe—56 men killed and wounded on board the Saratoga—Commodore Macdonough himself was three different times knocked down by the splinters and falling spars and blocks, but has escaped with trifling injury. The loss on either side it is difficult and as yet impossible to ascertain.

"The comparative loss to the enemy with ours is stated at two to one.

"The British fleet consisted of fifteen vessels, viz.:—

The Confiance, mounting, ...	39 guns.
Linnet, mounting, ...	16 guns.
Chub, mounting, ...	11 guns.
Finch, mounting, ...	11 guns.
11 Gallies, mounting, ...	16 guns.
	93 guns.

"Our fleet of fourteen vessels, viz.:—

Saratoga, ...	26
Eagle, ...	20
Ticonderoga, ...	17
Com. Preble, ...	7
6 Gallies, 2 each, ...	12
4 Gallies, 1 each, ...	4
	86

"On the result of this most glorious victory comment is unnecessary. The names of Macdonough and of his gallant officers, will be inserted among those of Decatur, Hull, Perry, Bainbridge, Porter, and Jones, and like them will be held in everlasting remembrance.

"The enemy under Sir George Prevost amounting to 14,000 regulars and embodied militia, in four brigades commanded by Major Generals De Rottenburgh, Powers, Brisbane, and Robinson, appeared before our works at Plattsburgh, and after bombarding, cannonading, and rocket-firing were obliged to retreat in the night of Sunday last, in great confusion, leaving a number of their tents, several pieces cannon, great quantities of ammunition, bombs, cannon balls, grape shot, fixed cartridges, shovels, spades, axes, pick axes, bread, flour, beef, etc., etc., in our possession, together with all their sick and wounded to our mercy. The gallantry of General Macomb, his subalterns and brave regulars (not exceeding 1,500), have never been exceeded. Not a pallid cheek was seen during the whole affair, notwithstanding the showers of shot, shells and rockets which were directed at our works. On silencing the enemy's battery the second time, Sir George made his escape with his life guard, while we were playing the tune of Yankee Doodle.

" The militia, thirty-two hundred, without distinction of party or age, in every instance have distinguished themselves. The Vermont volunteers have behaved with the coolness of regulars, and their conduct has fulfilled the expectations, which the promptness and spirit with which they turned out had raised.

" The enemy in their flight destroyed all the bridges and obstructed the road by trees, baggage, etc. They were however pursued as far as Chazy, but on account of the obstructions of the road and their precipient retreat, our *heroes* were not able to overtake them. The enemy have learnt a lesson long to be remembered, that the ' soil of Freedom is sacred, that it must not, shall not, be polluted with impunity.' In this their expedition by land and water, we can account to Sir George for more than *two thousand* of his men killed and prisoners, and more than *ninety* pieces of cannon.

" *To the interposition of heaven, be ascribed our glorious victory.*"

BRITISH ACCOUNT FROM THE MONTREAL "HERALD" OF SEPTEMBER 17, 1814

*

"Particulars of, the Late Disastrous Affair on Lake Champlain

"The brave and lamented Captain Downie, in the Confiance, led our small flotilla in battle in a gallant style, and as far as talents, the valor of British tars, and enthusiastic devotion to their country, could command victory, the most successful event was reasonably expected. That noble officer fell in his country's cause, the second shot, but his place was ably filled by his Lieut. who continued the engagement with unabated vigor, and was in the act of laying alongside the largest ship of the enemy, when the rudder of the Confiance was unshipped by a shot from the enemy. The Linnet, a small brig, which with the Confiance, was the only vessel of any size in our flotilla, went ashore; in this state lying like a log on the water, the Confiance maintained the unequal contest with the whole flotilla of the enemy, in which were 4 vessels of large size. History produces nothing superior to the valor and gallantry of the officers and crew of the Confiance; suffice it to say that she was literally fought to the water's edge; and if accounts are true, there remained but thirty of her men unhurt at the end of 5 hours' fighting. Such men will bring down the Americans, as their fathers heretofore have done the Dutch, who without disparagement, were at one time better sailors than our unnatural foe. Would that a veil could be drawn over the scene on shore! but it must afford a sad tale in the page of British history! The scientific, brave Generals, Officers, and soldiers of the Duke of Wellington's army, and the others who have before fought in our cause in the Canadas, did everything which depended on them to support the noble efforts of their brothers on the water. That distinguished officer, General Robinson, who has been twice wounded this year on the other continent, with part of his brigade, had braved all danger in an assault. Some of the picquet Fort were heretofore away, and a few minutes more would have given up the fortifications, with an immense train of artillery into our hands, and every American must have fallen, or been made prisoners. It was thought necessary to check the ardor of the troops, and we must now instantly redouble our energies to obtain the command of the Lake, or with humility await our future destiny."

EXTRACTS FROM GENERAL ORDERS ISSUED BY GEN. ALEX. MACOMB, AT PLATTSBURGH, SEPTEMBER 14, 1814

"The Governor General of the Canadas and Commander in Chief of the British forces in North America, having invaded the Territories of the United States, with the avowed purpose of conquering the country as far as Crown Point and Ticonderoga, there to winter his forces with a view to further conquest, brought with him a powerful army and flotilla,—an army amounting to fourteen thousand men, completely equipped and accompanied by a numerous train of artillery and all the engines of war,—men who had conquered in France, Spain, Portugal, the Indies, and in various other parts of the Globe, and led by the most distinguished Generals of the British army. A flotilla also, superior to ours in vessels, men, and guns, had determined at once to crush us both by land and by water.

"The Governor General * * * appeared before the village of Plattsburgh, with his whole army, and on the eleventh, the day fixed for the general attack, the flotilla arrived.

" The enemy's flotilla at 8 in the morning passed Cumberland Head, and at 9 engaged our flotilla at anchor in the bay off the town, fully confident of crushing in an instant the whole of our naval force; but our gallant Commodore Macdonough in the short space of two hours, obliged the large vessels to strike their colors, whilst the gallies saved themselves by flight. This glorious achievement was in full view of the several forts, and the American forces had the satisfaction of witnessing the Victory. The British army was also posted on the surrounding heights, that it could not but behold the interesting struggle for dominion on the Lake. At the same hour the fleets engaged, the enemy opened his batteries on our Forts, throwing hundreds of shells, balls and rockets and attempted at the same time to cross the Saranack at three different points to assault the works. At the upper ford he was met by the Militia and Volunteers, and after repeated attempts was driven back with considerable loss in killed, wounded and prisoners. At the Bridge near the Village he was repulsed by the pickets and brave riflemen under Captain Grovenor and Lts. Hamilton and Riley, and at the Bridge in the town, he was foiled by the guards, Block Houses, and the Artillery of the forts, served by Capt. Alexander Brooks, Capts. Richards and Smith, and Lieuts. Mountford, Smyth and Cromwell. The enemy's fire was returned with effect from our batteries and by sunset we had the satisfaction to silence seven batteries which he had erected, and to see his column retiring to their camps, beyond the reach of our guns.

"Thus beaten by land and by water, the Governor General withdrew his Artillery and raised the siege; at 9 at night sent off his heavy baggage and under cover of darkness, retreated with his whole army towards Canada, leaving his wounded on the field, and a vast quantity of bread, flour and beef which he had not time to destroy, besides a quantity of bombshells, shot, flints and ammunition of all kinds, which remain at the batteries and lie concealed in the ponds and rivers. As soon as his retreat was discovered the Light troops, Volunteers and Militia, were in pursuit, and followed as far as Chazy, capturing several dragoons and soldiers, besides covering the escape of hundreds of deserters, who continue still to be coming in. A violent storm and continual fall of rain prevented the brave Volunteers and Militia from further pursuit.

"Thus have the attempts of the invaders been frustrated by a regular force of only fifteen hundred men, a brave and active body of Militia of the State of New York, under Gen. Mooers, and Volunteers of the respectable and patriotic citizens of Vermont, led by Gen. Strong and other gentlemen of distinction, the whole not exceeding two thousand five hundred men.

"The British forces being now either expelled or captured, the services of the Volunteers and Militia may be dispensed with.

"General Macomb cannot however permit the Militia of New York and the Volunteers of Vermont, to depart without carrying with them the high sense he entertains for their merits. The zeal with which they came forward in defence of their Country, when the signal of danger was given by the General, reflects the highest lustre on their patriotism and spirit. * * *

"The General, in the name of the United States, thanks the Volunteers and the Militia for their distinguished services, and wishes them a happy return to their families and friends."

COMMODORE MACDONOUGH'S OFFICIAL REPORTS

United States' ship Saratoga, off
Plattsburgh, Sept. 11, 1814.

Sir: The Almighty has been pleased to grant us a signal victory on Lake Champlain, in the capture of one frigate, one brig, and two sloops of war of the enemy.

I have the honor to be,
Very respectfully sir,
Your obedient servant,
T. MACDONOUGH, Com.

Hon. William Jones, secretary of the navy.

United States' ship Saratoga, at anchor off
Plattsburgh, Sept. 13, 1814.

Sir: By Lieut. Commandant Cassin I have the honor to convey to you the flags of his Brittannic majesty's late squadron, captured on the 11th inst. by the United States' squadron, under my command. Also, my despatches relating to that occurrence, which should have been in your possession at an earlier period, but for the difficulty in arranging the different statements.

The squadron under my command now lies at Plattsburgh,—it will bear of considerable diminution, and leave a force sufficient to repel any attempt of the enemy in this quarter. I shall wait your order what to do with the whole or any part thereof, and should it be consistent, I beg you will favor me with permission to leave the lake and place me under command of Commodore Decatur, at New York. My health (being some time on the lake), together with the almost certain inactivity of future naval operations here, are among the causes for this request of my removal.

I have the honor to be,

Sir, with much respect,

Your most obedient servant,

T. MACDONOUGH.

Hon. William Jones, secretary of the navy, Washington.

United States' ship Saratoga,

Plattsburgh Bay, Sept. 11, 1814.

Sir: I have the honor to give you the particulars of the action which took place on the 11th inst. on this lake.

For several days the enemy were on their way to Plattsburgh, by land and water; and it being understood that an attack would be made at the same time by their land and naval forces, I determined to await at anchor the approach of the latter.

At 8 A. M. the lookout boat announced the approach of the enemy. At 9 he anchored in a line ahead, at about 300 yards distance from my line; his ship opposed to the Saratoga, his brig to the Eagle, Captain Robert Henley, his galleys, thirteen in number, to the schooner, sloop, and a division of our galleys: one of his sloops assisting their ship and brig, the other assisting their galleys. Our remaining galleys with the Saratoga and Eagle. In this situation, the whole force, on both sides, became engaged: the Saratoga suffering much from the heavy fire of the Confiance. I could perceive at the same time, however, that our fire was very destructive to her. The Ticonderoga, Lieut. Commandant Cassin, gallantly sustained her full share of the action. At half past 10 o'clock, the Eagle, not being able to bring her guns to bear, cut her cable, and anchored in a more eligible position, between my ship and the Ticonderoga, where she very much annoyed the enemy, but unfortunately leaving me exposed to a galling fire from the enemy's brig. Our guns on the starboard side being nearly all dismounted, or not manageable, a stern anchor was let go, the bower cable cut, and the ship winded with a fresh broadside on the enemy's ship, which soon after surrendered. Our broadside was then sprung to bear on the brig, which surrendered in about 15 minutes after.

The sloop that was opposed to the Eagle had struck some time before, and drifted down the line; the sloop which was with their galleys having struck also; three of their galleys are said to be sunk, the others pulled off. Our galleys were about obeying, with alacrity, the signal to follow them, when all the vessels were reported to me to be in a sinking state; it then became necessary to annul the signal to the galleys, and order their men to the pumps.

I could only look at the enemy's galleys going off in a shattered condition, for there was not a mast in either squadron that could stand to make sail on; the lower rigging, being nearly all shot away, hung down as though it had been just placed over the mast heads.

The Saratoga had fifty-five rounds shot in her hull; the Confiance one hundred and five. The enemy's shot passed principally just over our heads, as there were not twenty whole hammocks in the nettings at the close of the action, which lasted, without intermission, two hours and twenty minutes.

The absence and sickness of Lieut. Raymond Perry, left me without the services of that excellent officer; much ought fairly to be attributed to him for his great care and attention in disciplining the ship's crew, s her first lieutenant. His place was filled by a gallant young officer, Lieut. Peter Gamble, who I regret to inform you, was killed early in the action. Acting Lieut. Vallette worked the 1st and 2d divisions of guns with able effect. Sailing Master Brum's attention to the springs, and in the execution of the order to wind the ship, and occasionally at the guns, meets with my entire approbation; also Captain Young's commanding the acting marines, who took his men to the guns. Mr. Beale, purser, was of great service at the guns and in carrying my orders throughout the ship, with Midshipman Montgomery. Master's Mate, Joshua Justin, had the command of the third division: his conduct during the action was that of a brave and correct officer. Midshipmen Monteath, Graham, Williamson, Platt, Thwing, and Acting Midshipman Baldwin, all behaved well, and gave evidence of their making valuable officers.

The Saratoga was twice set on fire by hot shot from the enemy's ship.

I close, sir, this communication with feelings of gratitude for the able support I received from every officer and man attached to the squadron which I have the honor to command.

> I have the honor to be,
> With great respect, sir,
> Your most obedient servant,
> T. MACDONOUGH.

Hon. William Jones, secretary of the navy.

P. S. Accompanying this is a list of killed and wounded, a list of the prisoners, and a precise statement of both forces engaged. Also letters from Captain Henley and Lieutenant Commandant Cassin.

> T. M.

Statement of the American force engaged on the 11th September, 1814.

Saratoga, 8 long 24-pounders; 6 42-pound carronades; 12 52-pound carronades. Total, 26 guns.

Eagle, 12 32-pound carronades and 8 long 12-pounders. Total, 20 guns.

Ticonderoga, 8 long 12-pounders; 4 18-pounders; 5 32-pound carronades. Total, 17 guns.

Preble, 7 long 9-pounders. Total, 7 guns.

TEN GALLEYS, VIZ.:—

Allen, 1 long 24-pr. and 1 18-pr. Columbiad, 2; Burrows, 1 long 24-pr. and 1 18-pr. Columbiad, 2; Borer, 1 long 24-pr. and 1 18-pr. Columbiad, 2; Nettle, 1 long 24-pr. and 1 18-pr. Columbiad, 2; Viper, 1 long 24-pr. and 1 18-pr. Columbiad, 2; Centipede, 1 long 24-pr. and 1 18-pr. Columbiad, 2; Ludlow, 1 long 12-pounder, 1; Wilmer, 1 long 12-pounder, 1; Alwyn, 1 long 12-pounder, 1; Ballard, 1 long 12-pounder, 1. Guns, 86.

RECAPITULATION.

Fourteen long 24-pounders, 6 42-pound carronades, 29 32-pound carronades, 12 long 18-pounders, 12 12-pounders, 7 9-pounders, 6 18-pound Columbiads. Total, 86 guns.

T. MACDONOUGH.

Statement of the enemy's force engaged on the 11th September, 1814:

Frigate Confiance, 27 long 24-pounders, 4 32-pound carronades, 6 24-pound carronades, 2 long 18-pounders, on b. deck. Total, 39 guns.

Brig Linnet, 16 long 12-pounders, 16; Sloop Chub,* 10 18-pound carronades, 1 long 6-pounder, 11; Finch,* 6 18-pound carronades, 1 18-pound Columbiad, 4 long 6-pounders, 11.

THIRTEEN GALLEYS, VIZ.:—

Sir James Yeo, 1 long 24-pounder and 1 32-pound carronade, 2; Sir George Prevost, 1 long 24-pounder and 1 32-pound carronade, 2; Sir Sidney Beckwith, 1 long 24-pounder and 1 32-pound carronade, 2; Broke, 1 long 18-pounder and 1 32-pound carronade, 2; Murray, 1 long 18-pounder and 1 18-pound carronade, 2; Wellington, 1 long 18-pounder and 1 18-pound carronade, 2; Tecumseh, 1 long 18-pounder and 1 18-pound carronade, 2; name unknown, 1 18-pounder and 1 18-pound carronade, 2; Drummond, 1 32-pound carronade, 1; Simcoe, 1 32-pound carronade, 1; unknown, 1 32-pound carronade, 1; unknown, 1 32-pound carronade, 1; unknown, 1 32-pound carronade, 1. Total, 95.

RECAPITULATION.

Thirty long 24-pounders, 7 long 18-pounders, 16 long 12-pounders, 5 long 6-pounders, 13 32-pound carronades, 6 24-pound carronades, 17 18-pound carronades, 1 18-pound Columbiad. Total, 95 guns.

T. MACDONOUGH.

United States' brig Eagle,
Plattsburgh, Sept. 12, 1814.

Sir: I am happy to inform you that all my officers and men acted bravely, and did their duty in the battle yesterday, with the enemy.

I shall have the pleasure of making a more particular representation

*These sloops were formerly the United States' Growler and Eagle.

of the respective merits of my gallant officers, to the honorable the secretary of the navy.

I have the honor to be,

Respectfully sir,

Your most obedient servant,

ROBERT HENLEY.

P. S. We had 31 round shot in our hull (mostly 24-pounders), four in our lower masts, and we were well peppered with grape. I enclose my boatswain's report.

R. H.

United States' Schooner Ticonderoga,

Plattsburgh Bay, Sept. 12, 1814.

Sir :

It is with pleasure I state, that every officer and man under my command, did their duty yesterday.

Yours respectfully,

STEPHEN CASSIN,

Lieutenant Commandant.

Commodore Thomas Macdonough.

United States' ship Saratoga,

Sept. 15, 1814, off Plattsburgh.

Sir :

As Providence has given into my command the squadron on Lake Champlain, of which you were (after the fall of Captain Downie) the commanding officer, I beg you will, after the able conflict you sustained, and evidence of determined valor you evinced on board his Britannic majesty's brig Linnet, until the necessity of her surrender, accept of your enclosed parole, not to serve against the United States, or their dependencies, until regularly exchanged.

I am, &c. &c.

T. MACDONOUGH.

To Captain Pring, royal navy.

MACDONOUGH'S OFFICIAL REPORT OF THE AMERICAN LOSSES AND
BRITISH PRISONERS.

United States' ship Saratoga,

September 13, 1814.

Sir: I have the honor to enclose you a list of the killed and wounded on board the different vessels of the squadron under your command in the action of the 11th inst.

It is impossible to ascertain correctly the loss of the enemy.   From the best information received from the British officers, from my own observations, and from various lists found on board the Confiance, I calculate the number of men on board of that ship at the commencement of the action, at 270, of whom 180, at least were killed and wounded; and on board the other captured vessels at least, 80 more, making in the whole, killed or wounded, 260.   This is doubtless short of the real number, as many were thrown overboard from the Confiance during the engagement.

The muster books must have been thrown overboard, or otherwise disposed of, as they are not to be found.

I am, sir, respectfully,

Your obedient servant,

GEORGE BEALE, JR., Purser.

Thomas Macdonough, esq., commanding United States' squadron on Lake Champlain.

RETURN OF KILLED AND WOUNDED ON BOARD THE UNITED STATES'
SQUADRON ON LAKE CHAMPLAIN, IN THE ENGAGEMENT WITH
THE BRITISH FLEET, ON THE 11TH OF SEPTEMBER, 1814.

SHIP SARATOGA.

KILLED.

Peter Gamble, lieutenant,
Thomas Butler, quarter gunner,
James Norberry, boatswain's mate,
Abraham Davis, quartermaster,
William Wyer, sailmaker,
William Brickell, seaman,
Peter Johnson, seaman,
John Coleman, seaman,
Benjamin Burrill, ordinary seaman,
Andrew Parmelee, ordinary seaman,
Peter Post, seaman,
David Bennett, seaman,
Ebenezer Johnson, seaman,
Joseph Couch, landsman,
Thomas Stevens, seaman,
Randall McDonald, ordinary seaman,
John White, ordinary seaman,
Samuel Smith, seaman,
Thomas Maloney, ordinary seaman,
Andrew Nelson, seaman,
John Sellack, seaman,
Peter Hanson, seaman,
Jacob Laraway, seaman,

Edward Moore, seaman,
Jerome Williams, ordinary seaman,
James Carlisle, marine,
John Smart, seaman,
Earl Hannemon, seaman,
Total, 28.

WOUNDED.

James M. Baldwin, acting midshipman,
Joseph Barron, pilot,
Robert Gary, quarter gunner,
George Cassin, quartermaster,
John Hollingsworth, seaman,
Thomas Robinson, seaman,
Purnall Smith, seaman,
John Ottiwell, seaman,
John Thompson, ordinary seaman,
William Tabee, ordinary seaman,
William Williams, ordinary seaman,
John Roberson, seaman,
John Towns, landsman,
John Shays, seaman,
John S. Hammond, seaman,
James Barlow, seaman,
James Nagle, ordinary seaman,
John Lanman, seaman,
Peter Colberg, seaman,
William Newton, ordinary seaman,
Neil J. Heidmont, seaman,

James Steward, seaman,
John Adams, landsman,
Charles Ratche, seaman,
Benjamin Jackson, marine,
Jesse Vanhorn, marine,
Joseph Ketter, marine,
Samuel Pearson, marine,
Total, 29.

BRIG EAGLE.

KILLED.

Peter Vandermere, master's mate,
John Ribero, seaman,
Jacob Lindman, seaman,
Perkins Moore, ordinary seaman,
James Winship, ordinary seaman,
Thomas Anwright, ordinary seaman,
Nace Wilson, ordinary seaman,
Thomas Lewis, boy,
John Wallace, marine,
Joseph Heaton, marine,
Robert Stratton, marine,
James M. Hale, musician,
John Wood, musician,
Total, 13.

WOUNDED.

Joseph Smith, lieutenant,
William A. Spencer, acting lieutenant,

Francis Breeze, master's mate,
Abraham Walters, pilot,
William C. Allen, quartermaster,
James Duick, quarter gunner,
Andrew McEwen, seaman,
Zebediah Conklin, seaman,
Joseph Valentine, seaman,
John Hartley, seaman,
John Micklan, seaman,
Robert Buckley, seaman,
Aaron Fitzgerald, boy,
Purnall Boice, ordinary seaman,
John N. Craig, seaman,
John McKenny, seaman,
Mathew Scriver, marine,
George Mainwaring, marine,
Henry Jones, marine,
John McCarty, marine,
Total, 20.

SCHOONER TICONDEROGA.

KILLED.

John Stansbury, lieutenant,
John Fisher, boatswain's mate,
John Atkinson, boatswain's mate,
Henry Johnson, seaman,
Deodrick Think, marine,
John Sharp, marine,
Total, 6.

WOUNDED.

Patrick Cassin, seaman,
Ezekiel Gould, seaman,
Samuel Sawyer, seaman,
William Le Count, seaman,
Henry Collin, seaman,
John Condon, marine,
Total, 6.

SLOOP PREBLE.

KILLED.

Rogers Carter, acting sailing master,
Joseph Rowe, boatswain's mate,

WOUNDED.

None.

GUNBOAT BORER.

KILLED.

Arthur W. Smith, purser's steward,
Thomas Gill, boy,
James Day, marine,

WOUNDED.

Ebenezer Cobb, corporal of marines,

GUNBOAT CENTIPEDE.

WOUNDED.

James Taylor, landsman,

GUNBOAT WILMER.

WOUNDED.

Peter Frank, seaman,

RECAPITULATION.

	Killed.	Wounded.
Saratoga	28	29
Eagle	13	20
Ticonderoga	6	6
Preble	2	—
Borer	3	1
Centipede	—	1
Wilmer	—	1
	52	58

Gunboats, Nettle, Allen, Viper, Burrows, Ludlow, Alwyn, Ballard,—none killed or wounded.

GEORGE BEALE, JR., Purser.

Approved,

T. MACDONOUGH.

LIST OF PRISONERS CAPTURED ON 11TH SEPTEMBER, AND SENT TO GREENBUSH.

OFFICERS.

Daniel Pring,* captain,

Hicks, lieutenant,

Creswick, lieutenant,

Robinson, lieutenant,

*On parole.

McGhie, lieutenant,

Drew, lieutenant,

Hornsby, lieutenant,

Childs, lieutenant marines,

Fitzpatrick, lieutenant 39th Regiment,

Bryden, sailing master,

Clark, master mate,

Simmonds, master mate,

Todd, surgeon,

Giles, purser,

Guy, captain clerk,

Dowell, midshipman,

Aire, midshipman,

Bondell, midshipman,

Toorke, midshipman,

Kewstra, midshipman,

Davidson, boatswain,

Elvin, gunner,

Mickel, gunner,

Cox, carpenter,

Parker, purser,

Martin, surgeon,

McCabe, assistant surgeon,

340 seamen,

47 wounded men paroled.

RECORD OF THE FORCE AND LOSS OF THE AMERICAN AND BRITISH FLEETS SENT BY COMMODORE MACDONOUGH TO A CITIZEN OF BURLINGTON, VT.

*

AMERICAN.

	Guns.	Men.	Killed.	Wounded.
Saratoga, ship,	26	210	26	20
Eagle, brig,	20	120	13	27
Ticonderoga, schooner,	17	110	6	6
Preble, sloop,	7	30	1	1
10 Gunboats,	16	350	3	3
Totals,	86	820	49	57

The American officers killed were Lieutenants Gamble and Stansbury, and Sailing Master Carter.

ENGLISH.

	Guns.	Men.	Killed.	Wounded.
Large ship,	39	300	50	60
Brig,	16	120	20	30
Sloop, formerly Growler,	11	40	6	10
Sloop, formerly Eagle,	11	40	8	10
11 Gunboats,	16	550	2 probably sunk.	
Totals,	93	1050	84	110

The British officers killed were Commodore Downie, Captain Pring, and six or eight lieutenants. The wounded were paroled and sent by vessel to the Isle aux Noix.

OFFICERS OF THE UNITED STATES
ARMY STATIONED AT BUR-
LINGTON, VT., MAY 20, 1814.

OFFICERS OF THE UNITED STATES ARMY STATIONED AT BURLINGTON, VT., MAY 20, 1814.

George McFeely, lieutenant-colonel, 22nd Infantry,
Samuel Gilliland, surgeon, 16th Infantry,
John Pentland, captain, 22nd Infantry,
James F. McElnay, captain, 16th Infantry,
William Davenport, captain, 16th Infantry,
Joseph L. Barton, captain, 15th Infantry,
Miles Greenwood, captain, 16th Infantry,
John D. Coon, captain, 16th Infantry,
Thomas M. Powers, lieutenant and paymaster, 16th Infantry,
John Sacket, surgeon's mate, 11th Infantry,
Alexander Macomb, brigadier-general, United States Army,
Elias Fassett, colonel, 30th Infantry,
White Youngs, captain, 15th Infantry,
Henry Van Dalsen, captain, 15th Infantry,
Robert T. Baker, surgeon's mate, 15th Infantry,
Benjamin Branch, captain, Light Artillery,
John M. O'Connor, captain, Artillery,
Willis Foulk, captain, 22nd Infantry,
William R. Duncan, lieutenant of Artillery and brigade major,
George W. Ferguson, lieutenant, 22nd Infantry,
R. E. De Ruffey, lieutenant, United States engineers,
Thomas C. Walker, hospital surgeon's mate,
Abraham Godwin, lieutenant, 15th Infantry,
William Sturgis, lieutenant, 22nd Infantry,
Jacob Whisler, lieutenant and adjutant, 16th Infantry,

Henry K. Mullin, lieutenant, 15th Infantry,
Joseph Wallace, hospital surgeon's mate,
William Barney, lieutenant, 30th Infantry,
Isaac Finch, lieutenant, 16th Infantry,
Thomas Evans, lieutenant, 16th Infantry,
A. Bostwick, lieutenant, 30th Infantry,
John Trevitt, garrison surgeon's mate,
Charles H. Roberts, lieutenant, 15th Infantry,
Florant Merine, lieutenant, 15th Infantry,
Joseph Scofield, lieutenant, 15th Infantry
Joseph P. Russell, acting surgeon's mate,
Nelson Freeland, lieutenant, Light Artillery,
Thomas Lyon, lieutenant, 16th Infantry,
William B. Howell, lieutenant, 15th Infantry,
Samuel Nicholson, lieutenant, 16th Infantry,
Robert B. Beans, ensign, 22nd Infantry,
J. L. Burton, lieutenant and adjutant, 30th Infantry,
John S. Grant, ensign, 15th Infantry,
William Coffie, lieutenant and quartermaster,15th Infantry,
John Rose, lieutenant, 15th Infantry,
Daniel E. Burch, lieutenant and paymaster, 15th Infantry,
Levi Heath, lieutenant, 15th Infantry,
J. Y. M'Kinney, lieutenant, Light Artillery,
Richard W. Field, lieutenant, Light Artillery,
James White, ensign, 16th Infantry,
Henry Stanton, captain and assistant district quartermaster-gen-
    eral,
Henry Huntt, hospital surgeon,
John Armstrong, lieutenant, 22nd Infantry,
Charles F. Hennings, ensign, 22nd Infantry,
Charles Fisler, lieutenant, 16th Infantry,
Æneas Mackay, lieutenant, United States Ordnance,
Samuel McDougall, lieutenant, 15th Infantry,

A. W. Thornton, captain, Light Artillery,
Samuel Riddle, lieutenant, 15th Infantry,
J. H. Wilkins, lieutenant, Light Artillery,
Walter Sheldon, lieutenant and assistant paymaster,
Thomas Lawrence, captain, 16th Infantry,
William B. Ferriss, ensign, 30th Infantry,
Joseph E. Merritt, assistant district paymaster.

ABSTRACTS FROM PAYROLLS OF REGIMENTS STATIONED AT BURLINGTON, VT., DURING THE WAR OF 1812.

WHERE MORE THAN ONE ROLL OF A COMPANY IS GIVEN, ONLY THE ADDED NAMES ARE PRINTED.

PAY ROLL OF A COMPANY OF INFANTRY COM-
MANDED BY CAPTAIN BENJAMIN S. EDGER-
TON, OF THE ELEVENTH REGIMENT OF
THE UNITED STATES, FOR THE
MONTHS OF SEPTEMBER AND
OCTOBER, 1812.

Benjamin S. Edgerton, captain,
William S. Heaton, second lieutenant,
Fred A. Sawyer, ensign,
Joshua P. Burnham, sergeant,
Ebenezer W. Bohonnon, sergeant,
Benjamin G. Houston, sergeant,
Nathan Young, sergeant,
Bizaleel Bradford, corporal,
Silas C. McClary, corporal,
Harry B. Webster, corporal,
Joseph N. Sanborn, musician,
Elijah Bigelow, private,
Eretus Belding, private,
William Briggs, private,
William Bert, private,
Reuben A. Buswell, private, died Jan. 3, 1813,
Thomas Burks, private,
Andrew Bradford, private,
John W. Cuthburt, private,
Joseph J. Chamberlin, private,

Cyrus Chamberlin, private,
Jonathan Clark, private,
Solomon Clark, private,
Elanson S. Cogswell, private,
James Cummings, private,
Samuel J. Cleveland, private,
John J. Collins, private,
Cushman Downer, private,
John Desau, private,
David French, private,
Otis Franklin, private,
John L. Fisher, private,
Abel Fletcher, private,
Baptist Flemming, private,
James J. Grimes, private,
John Hall, private,
Moses Hall, private,
Obededam Hall, private,
Antipart D. Hall, private,
Eleazer Hawes, private,
Levi Hicks, private, died Jan. 26, 1813,
Thomas Houghton, private, deserted Feb. 1, 1813,
Ira Johnson, private,
David Jewett, private,
Simon Jones, private,
Amos Kyle, private,
Ephriam Leonard, private,
Horatio Lord, private,
Peter Lewin, private,
Robert Lewin, private,
Samuel McMaster, private,
Joseph Manor, private,
John Newton, private,

David Norris, private, deserted Jan. 28, 1813,
Thomas Nash, private,
Erasmus Osborn, private,
Joseph Orne, private,
Ebenezer Orne, private,
Francis Pilkey, private,
William Phillips, private,
Samuel Ransom, private,
Ami R. C. Ransom, private,
Nathan Richardson, private,
Jedidiah H. Robertson, private,
Isaac Robertson, private,
Jarvis Randall, private,
Alfred Sloan, private,
Elisha Sawyer, private,
Reuben Strong, private,
Ebenezer White, private,
Daniel Weed, private, died Feb. 21, 1813,
Daniel Woodbury, private,
James Weaver, private.

PAYROLL OF CAPTAIN BENJAMIN S. EDGERTON'S COMPANY FOR
THE MONTHS OF JANUARY AND FEBRUARY, 1813.

Horace Hale, first lieutenant,
Abial Whiting, musician,
James Bassett, private,
Moses Church, private, died March 2, 1813,
John Dean, private,
Joseph Ellery, private,
Anson Frazier, private,
Richard Griffin, private,
James Griffin, private,
Daniel Griffin, private,

Joshua Hyde, private, died Sept. 19, 1813,
John Hyde, private,
Beals Kitticut, private,
Clement S. Miner, private,
John Moody, private,
Amos Phillips, private,
Hewe Platt, private,
Charles H. Stacy, private,
Roderick Taylor, private,
Edward L. Wilson, private, deserted Feb. 27, 1813.

PAYROLL OF CAPTAIN BENJAMIN S. EDGERTON'S COMPANY,

MAY 31, 1813.

John Arlin, private, enlisted Feb. 2, 1813,
Henry Allard, private, enlisted Feb. 19, 1813,
Jacob Allard, private, enlisted March 1, 1813,
John Blanchard, private, enlisted March 26, 1813,
Gates Blanchard, private, enlisted Dec. 30, 1812,
John O. Brown, private, enlisted March 2, 1813,
John Bolles, private, enlisted March 22, 1813,
Benjamin Brown, private, enlisted Feb. 20, 1813,
Andrew Brewer, private, enlisted Feb. 8, 1813, deserted
    Feb. 27, 1813,
Daniel Cross, private, enlisted Feb. 13, 1813,
Cheeny Coburn, private, enlisted Feb. 13, 1813,
Elam Clark, private, enlisted Jan. 9, 1813,
George Conant, private, enlisted March 5, 1813,
John Chamberlain, private, enlisted March 10, 1813,
Ebenezer Chamberlain, private, enlisted March 17, 1813,
Aaron Caldwell, private, enlisted March 31, 1813,
Love Dennet, private, enlisted March 5, 1813,
Israel Dagget, private, enlisted Jan. 15, 1813,

Calvin Edson, private, enlisted March 25, 1813,

Alden Farnsworth, private, enlisted Feb. 11, 1813,

Charles Fox, private, enlisted March 17, 1813,

John Greene, private, enlisted Feb. 15, 1813,

Joseph Goolet, private, enlisted Jan. 14, 1813,

John Giles, private, enlisted March 9, 1813,

John Goodwin, private, enlisted March 4, 1813,

John B. Hibbard, private, enlisted Jan. 18, 1813,

Eli Hynds, private, enlisted March 12, 1813,

Samuel Hawkins, private, enlisted Feb. 23, 1813,

Tracy Harris, private, enlisted Feb. 9, 1813, died May
    18, 1813,

Mansel Haselton, private, enlisted March 29, 1813,

Nathan Hinds, private, enlisted March 12, 1813,

John F. John, private, enlisted April 7, 1813,

Christopher John, private, enlisted April 7, 1813,

William Keyes, private, enlisted March 29, 1813,

David Lathe, private, enlisted Feb. 11, 1813,

Enoch Little, private, enlisted April 7, 1813,

Calvin Morse, private, enlisted March 5, 1813,

James Myers, private, enlisted March 9, 1813,

John McNally, private, enlisted March 10, 1813,

John Nichols, private, enlisted March 22, 1813,

Elisha Norton, private, enlisted March 23, 1813,

Augustus Place, private, enlisted March 26, 1813,

Sanford Place, private, enlisted March 26, 1813,

Nicholas Pierce, private, enlisted Feb. 13, 1813, desert-
    ed in March, 1813,

John Palmer, private, enlisted Feb. 19, 1813,

James Pingree, private, enlisted Feb. 16, 1813,

Shadrack Place, private, enlisted March 3, 1813,

William Richardson, private, enlisted Feb. 11, 1813,

Joel S. Richardson, private, enlisted Feb. 11, 1813,

Nathan Stearns, private, enlisted Feb. 12, 1813,

Aaron Scott, private, enlisted Feb. 11, 1813,
Nathaniel Sias, private, enlisted March 4, 1813,
Luther Stockwell, private, enlisted March 27, 1813,
Joseph Smith, private, enlisted Feb. 18, 1813,
Putnam Silver, private, enlisted Feb. 27, 1813,
Levi Smith, private, enlisted March 8, 1813,
Thomas W. Steward, private, enlisted March 22, 1813,
      deserted March 25, 1813,
Christopher Silver, private, enlisted March 27, 1813,
Zebediah Silver, private, enlisted March 29, 1813,
Jotham Stevens, private, enlisted April 5, 1813,
Henry Skinner, private, enlisted March 11, 1813,
Bernice Snow, private, enlisted March 17, 1813,
Samuel Stacpole, private, enlisted Jan. 1, 1813,
Abram Thayer, private, enlisted March 15, 1813,
Paul Varney, private, enlisted March 29, 1813,
John Whitney, private, enlisted March 2, 1813,
Nathaniel Walker, private, enlisted Feb. 25, 1813,
Rufus Whitcomb, private, enlisted Feb. 22, 1813,
Nicholas C. Wells, private, enlisted Feb. 12, 1813,
Sylvester Washburn, private, enlisted April 2, 1813,
Samuel Wiley, private, enlisted Feb. 13, 1813,
Robert Willson, private, enlisted Feb. 15, 1813, desert-
      ed March 2, 1813.

PAYROLL OF A COMPANY OF INFANTRY COM-
MANDED BY CAPTAIN SAMUEL H. HOLLEY,
OF THE ELEVENTH REGIMENT OF THE
UNITED STATES, FOR THE MONTHS
OF JANUARY AND FEBRUARY, 1813.

Samuel H. Holley, captain,
Rufus Hatch, first lieutenant and assistant deputy
    quartermaster,
Walter Sheldon, second lieutenant and paymaster of
    the Eleventh Regiment,
William F. Haile, ensign,
Charles Backus, sergeant,
Enoch Cooper, sergeant,
Leonard Hawes, sergeant,
Philo Perry, sergeant,
M. De La F. Rogers, sergeant,
Isaiah Goodno, corporal,
David Price, corporal,
John Reed, corporal,
Calvin Stewart, corporal,
Josiah W. Knight, musician,
Nathaniel Parker, musician,
Jacob Aldrich, private,
Ebenezer Aldrich, private,
Elisha R. Allen, private,
Solomon B. Burbank, private,
John Bell, private,

David Blanchard, private,
David J. Benson, private,
Jonathan J. Belding, private,
Calvin Bingham, private,
Henry Burgess, private,
Daniel Beals, private,
Moses Baker, private,
James T. Bingham, private,
Joseph Bingham, private,
Jeremiah Bingham, second, private,
Joseph H. Bryant, private,
John Dantz, private,
David Dickey, private,
Jason Eager, private,
Hiram Eager, private,
Moses Emerson, private,
ʻOdel Flemming, private,
Chancey Fose, private,
Silas B. Fisher, private,
Noah Goodrich, private,
Joshua Graves, private,
Edward Green, private,
Ebenezer Green, private,
James Gomans, private, died Feb. 19, 1813,
Oliver C. Hicok, private,
Benjamin J. Holley, private,
Ezra Hamlin, private,
Nathaniel B. Harvey, private,
Joseph Hudson, private,
Marcus D. Hewit, private,
Israel Hewit, private,
Hubbard D. Hill, private, died Feb. 10, 1813,
William H. Judd, private,

Charles Killam, private,
William Kellogg, private,
Nathaniel Knight, private,
Abraham Lapman, private,
David Linsley, private,
Jonathan Lawrence, private,
Amos S. Mills, private,
Ellis Manham, private,
Jonathan Mosier, private,
Thomas J. Mills, private,
Bohon S. Monro, private,
Peter Myers, private,
Joseph B. Neal, private,
Amasa Owen, private,
John Powers, private,
John Price, private,
Russell P. Rogers, private,
Ezekiel Rogers, private,
Seth L. Robins, private,
Aaron Rumsay, private,
Ebenezer Reynolds, private,
John Rowley, private,
Hazad Shaw, private,
Lewis Smith, private,
Eli Snow, private,
Druses Shumway, private,
Nathan Stoddard, private,
Samuel G. Sumner, private,
Eliakin Sprague, private,
Jeremiah Sprague, private,
Horatio Sprague, private,
Jason Thaier, private,
Artimus Tyler, private,

John B. Tyler, private,
John Thompson, private,
Nathan Tuttle, private,
Horace B. Tower, private,
Abiathar Wheeler, private,
Joseph J. Walbridge, private,
Caleb A. Welton, private,
Joseph Wallace, private,
Elias Whaley, private,
Samuel Wilbur, private,
Phineas Whitney, private,
Harman B. Warren, private,
Cato Williams, private.

PAYROLL OF A COMPANY OF INFANTRY, COM-
MANDED BY CAPTAIN CHARLES FOLLETT,
OF THE ELEVENTH REGIMENT OF THE
UNITED STATES, FOR THE MONTHS OF
JANUARY AND FEBRUARY, 1813.

Charles Follett, captain,
Benjamin Smead, first lieutenant,
Henry T. Blake, second lieutenant,
Ansell Birge, sergeant,
John Hooper, sergeant,
Hiram Harwood, sergeant,
Smith Newcomb, sergeant,
Frederick Tiffany, sergeant,
Caleb Bailey, corporal, enlisted Jan. 26, 1813,
David Brown, corporal, discharged Jan. 26, 1813,
Thomas Coats, corporal,
Noah French, corporal, enlisted Feb. 6, 1813,
Jethro Smith, corporal,
Joseph Marsh, musician,
Isaac Billings, private,
Daniel Christie, private,
Simeon Cook, private,
David Drain, private,
Jesse Eldred, private,
James Fisher, private,
Daniel French, private,

William Fairfield, private,
Liberty Goodnough, private, died Jan. 22, 1813,
Thomas Harris, private,
Peter Jewett, private,
George W. King, private,
Joseph Knowles, private,
Charles C. Lane, private,
Chillon W. Lackey, private,
Thomas Low, private,
William Marston, private,
Amasa McCoy, private,
John Oatman, private,
Simon Pelot, private, enlisted Feb. 9, 1813,
Elihu Riddle, private,
James P. Seaton, private, died Feb. 26, 1813,
Henry Sumrix, private,
Ephraim Walker, private,
Richard Washburn, private,

PAYROLL OF CAPTAIN CHARLES FOLLETT'S COMPANY, MAY
31, 1813.

Melzar B. Buck, sergeant, enlisted April 1, 1813,
Jared Sears, sergeant, enlisted Feb. 22, 1813,
Nathan Thompson, sergeant, enlisted Feb. 20, 1813,
Samuel Thompson, sergeant, enlisted Feb. 20, 1813,
Thomas Tupper, sergeant, enlisted April 15, 1813,
Ira Doty, corporal, enlisted Feb. 25, 1813,
Oliver Pomeroy, corporal, enlisted Feb. 18, 1813,
Elisha Taylor, corporal, enlisted March 20, 1813,
Isaac Bullis, fifer, enlisted March 9, 1813,
Lyman Hall, fifer, enlisted March 27, 1813,
Valentine Parmenter, drummer, enlisted April 2, 1813,
John W. Anderson, private, enlisted Feb. 17, 1813,
Seth Andrus, private, enlisted March 18, 1813,

Simeon Atwater, private, enlisted March 24, 1813,
Joel Bixby, private, enlisted Feb. 15, 1813,
Jonathan Baker, private, enlisted Feb. 7, 1813,
Benjamin Blanchar, private, enlisted March 9, 1813,
Salmon Brown, private, enlisted March 15, 1813,
Warren Brown, private, enlisted March 13, 1813,
Ephriam Brown, private, enlisted March 15, 1813,
Aaron Bissell, private, enlisted March 25, 1813,
Joseph Bulliss, private, enlisted April 9, 1813,
John Bulliss, private, enlisted April 5, 1813,
Archibald Black, private, enlisted March 13, 1813,
Stephen Barnard, private, enlisted Feb. 9, 1813,
David Ball, private, enlisted March 6, 1813,
Leonard Butler, private, enlisted March 11, 1813,
Jonathan Bailey, private, enlisted March 16, 1813,
Marshall Blaisdell, private, enlisted April 24, 1813,
Reuben Beebe, private, enlisted Feb. 24, 1813,
John Barrett, private, enlisted March 10, 1813,
Nathaniel Brown, private, enlisted Feb. 8, 1813,
James Brown, private, enlisted Jan. 7, 1813,
Timothy Blake, private, enlisted Jan. 8, 1813,
Harvey D. Blake, private, enlisted Jan. 8, 1813,
David Blake, private, enlisted Jan. 11, 1813,
David Church, private, enlisted Sept. 27, 1812,
Shuball Cook, private, enlisted March 30, 1813,
Jonas Cutter, private, enlisted Feb. 2, 1813, died Feb. 2,
    1813,
Archibald Curry, private, enlisted March 13, 1813, died
    April 5, 1813,
Samuel Couch, private, enlisted March 20, 1813,
Jarvill Chaffee, private, enlisted March 20, 1813,
Isaac Clark, private, enlisted Feb. 15, 1813,
John Congdon, private, enlisted March 27, 1813,

Martin Cooley, private, enlisted March 27, 1813,
Peter Carvey, private, enlisted March 16, 1813,
Rufus Coller, private, enlisted Feb. 9, 1813,
George Dennis, private, enlisted Feb. 25, 1813,
Peter Darling, private, enlisted Feb. 27, 1813,
Benjamin Davis, private, enlisted March 18, 1813,
John Dewey, private, enlisted April 6, 1813,
Daniel Drain, private, enlisted Feb. 8, 1813,
Abijah Eaton, private, enlisted Feb. 22, 1813,
Joseph Emery, private, enlisted Feb. 15, 1813,
Erastus Fling, private, enlisted Feb. 13, 1813,
Josiah Folsom, private, enlisted March 13, 1813,
Noah Finch, private, enlisted Feb. 5, 1813,
Thomas Farrand, private, enlisted March 3, 1813,
Stephen French, private, enlisted Feb. 23, 1813, deserted
    April 14, 1813,
James Food, private, enlisted March 17, 1813,
James Fordham, private, enlisted Feb. 9, 1813,
William Fuller, private, enlisted Jan. 22, 1813,
Silent Graves, private, enlisted March 22, 1813,
Ephraim Garvin, private, enlisted March 30, 1813,
Elisha Griswold, private, enlisted Feb. 20, 1813,
John Glynn, private, enlisted March 3, 1813,
Jonathan Hunter, private, enlisted Feb. 13, 1813,
Minord Hilyard, private, enlisted Feb. 23, 1813,
John Harris, private, enlisted March 9, 1813,
Smith Headen, private, enlisted March 19, 1813,
David Hines, private, enlisted March 11, 1813,
Sylvester Holdridge, private, enlisted March 17, 1813,
Nathaniel Hall, private, enlisted Feb. 23, 1813,
Zenos Jones, private, enlisted March 4, 1813,
Zenos Jones, Jr., private, enlisted March 10, 1813,

John Low, private, enlisted Feb. 15, 1813, died March
   26, 1813,
Calvin Lewins, private, enlisted March 20, 1813,
Hezekiah A. Lambert, private, enlisted Feb. 20, 1813,
Ezekiel Leonard, private, enlisted March 19, 1813,
Samuel Lines, private, enlisted March 1, 1813,
Daniel McCollum, private, enlisted March 16, 1813,
Silas Moses, private, enlisted Feb. 26, 1813,
John Moses, private, enlisted Feb. 26, 1813,
Ibrook Miller, private, enlisted Feb. 14, 1813,
Dennis McBride, private, enlisted March 22, 1813,
Jeremiah Martin, private, enlisted March 20, 1813,
David Manchester, private, enlisted March 17, 1813,
John Nurse, private, enlisted March 27, 1813,
Nathaniel Oliver, private, enlisted March 4, 1813,
Stephen Purrington, private, enlisted March 20, 1813,
Ebenezer Pierce, private, enlisted Feb. 20, 1813,
John S. Post, private, enlisted March 27, 1813,
Simeon Pope, private, enlisted April 20, 1813,
John Ransellaer, private, enlisted March 8, 1813,
Moses Ransom, private, enlisted Feb. 17, 1813, died April
   20, 1813,
John Ross, private, enlisted Feb. 5, 1813,
Stephen Rice, private, enlisted Jan. 4, 1813,
Amos Randall, private, enlisted Feb. 17, 1813,
Thomas Robinson, private, enlisted March 10, 1813,
Patrick Roach, private, enlisted Feb. 13, 1813,
Asa Stiles, private, enlisted Feb. 16, 1813,
Reuben Stiles, private, enlisted Feb. 10, 1813,
Ezra Stiles, private, enlisted Feb. 17, 1813,
James Smith, private, enlisted Feb. 22, 1813,
Harry Smith, private, enlisted Jan. 24, 1813, died April
   22, 1813,

Alpheus Smith, private, enlisted March 12, 1813,

Enoch Smith, private, enlisted March 8, 1813,

Phineas Smith, private, enlisted Feb. 18, 1813, died April 24, 1813,

Solomon Sharp, private, enlisted Feb. 2, 1813,

Simeon Sanburn, private, enlisted March 12, 1813, died April 3, 1813,

Joseph Sumrix, private, enlisted Feb. 26, 1813,

William Smith, private, enlisted April 4, 1813,

Robert Stetson, private, enlisted Feb. 26, 1813,

John Tibbetts, private, enlisted Feb. 20, 1813,

Francis Thompson, private, enlisted March 29, 1813,

John Tinney, private, enlisted March 1, 1813,

John Titus, Jr., private, enlisted April 25, 1813,

John Withey, private, enlisted March 27, 1813,

Rixford Wittum, private, enlisted Feb. 4, 1813,

George Whitemor, private, enlisted March 8, 1813,

Jacob Wheeler, private, enlisted March 3, 1813,

Lewis Wright, private, enlisted April 4, 1813,

John Wait, Jr., private, enlisted Feb. 8, 1813,

Hamilton Williams, private, enlisted March 30, 1813, deserted March 30, 1813.

PAY ROLL OF A COMPANY OF INFANTRY COM-
MANDED BY CAPTAIN SAMUEL GORDON,
OF THE ELEVENTH REGIMENT OF THE
UNITED STATES, FOR THE MONTHS
OF JANUARY AND FEBRUARY,
1813.

Samuel Gordon, captain,
Rufus Bucklin, second lieutenant,
Thomas Staniford, ensign,
James Goodhue, sergeant, appointed quartermaster
    sergeant Feb. 11, 1813,
Ruben C. Hyde, sergeant,
Augustus Powers, sergeant,
Perez S. Sanford, sergeant,
Benjamin H. Tozer, sergeant,
Elijah Branch, corporal,
Elial Bond, corporal,
Oliver Emerson, corporal,
David Hartshorn, corporal,
Benjamin Rogers, corporal,
Mason Young, corporal,
Prentis Coats, musician,
Isaac Wright, musician,
John Ballard, private,
Isaac Brown, private,

Oliver Bugbee, private,
John Bishop, private, deserted in Aug., 1812, delivered himself up Sept. 1, 1812,
Simon Clark, private, died July 3, 1813,
John Collins, private, died July 5, 1813,
James T. Cook, private,
Thomas Davis, private,
Joel Densmore, private,
Amzi Dutton, private,
Jacob F. Eaton, private,
George Forbes, private,
Ruben Geddings, private,
Peter B. Goodrich, private,
Samuel E. Godfrey, private, confined in Vermont state prison,
Samuel Gibson, private,
George Jenne, private,
Francis Jefts, private,
David Jewil, private, died Feb. 17, 1813,
Sheldon Lockwood, private,
Alfred Leonard, private,
Lyman Leonard, private, died Jan. 5, 1813,
Silas Lovell, private,
Calvin S. Miller, private,
Stephen Maynard, private,
Guy Morgan, private,
William P. Morey, private,
Joseph Newman, private,
William Newman, private,
Erastus Norton, private,
Elisha Plumb, private,
Ezra Porter, private,
George Pelsue, private,

PAYROLL OF CAPTAIN SAMUEL GORDON'S COMPANY,
MAY 31, 1813.

D. W. Bates, corporal, enlisted March 8, 1813,
Horatio Emmons, corporal, enlisted March 14, 1813,
Simion Herrick, corporal, enlisted March 15, 1813,
Jarvis Hanks, musician, enlisted March 15, 1813,
Charles Bell, private, enlisted March 25, 1813,
Orlean Bell, private, enlisted Feb. 10, 1813,
James Bashford, private, enlisted March 29, 1813,
Ebenezer Brown, private, enlisted Feb. 17, 1813,
David Benson, private, enlisted April 14, 1813,
John Collins, private, enlisted Feb. 12, 1813, died March
     23, 1813,
Samuel Corliss, private, enlisted March 30, 1813,
Alexander Chase, private, enlisted March 11, 1813,
Josiah Conner, private, enlisted Feb. 11, 1813,
D. S. Cushman, private, enlisted March 25, 1813,
Elias Comb, private, enlisted March 29, 1813,
Asa Edmonds, private, enlisted March 25, 1813,
Jacob F. Eaton, private, enlisted Feb. 2, 1813,
John Fisk, private, enlisted March 11, 1813,
David Fuller, private, enlisted April 7, 1813,
Samuel Gibson, private, enlisted Feb. 8, 1813,
Thomas Goodwin, private, enlisted March 15, 1813,
Jonathan Goff, private, enlisted March 29, 1813,
Hezekiah Goff, private, enlisted March 29, 1813,
Abner Glines, private, enlisted March 13, 1813,
Martin Glines, private, enlisted March 13, 1813,
Moses Hatch, private, enlisted Feb. 12, 1813,
John Herriman, private, enlisted Jan. 21, 1813,
Uriah Higgins, private, enlisted March 24, 1813,
Asa Hill, private, enlisted April 14, 1813,

John Herrick, private, enlisted March 22, 1813,
John Hunt, private, enlisted March 10, 1813,
Abram Hobbs, private, enlisted March 16, 1813,
Eri Howe, private, enlisted March 6, 1813,
William S. Heath, private, enlisted Feb. 11, 1813,
Jeremiah Heath, private, enlisted Feb. 11, 1813,
Peter Heath, private, enlisted Feb. 11, 1813,
Elisha Hammond, private, enlisted Feb. 11, 1813,
John Lovell, private, enlisted Feb. 13, 1813,
Benjamin Linde, private, enlisted April 7, 1813,
John Mashee, private, enlisted March 9, 1813,
Jonathan B. Meritt, private, enlisted April 2, 1813,
I. W. Mighell, private, enlisted March 18, 1813,
David McCoy, private, enlisted April 13, 1813,
Moses Nichols, private, enlisted April 2, 1813,
Stephen Northrop, private, enlisted March 31, 1813,
Daniel Noyes, private, enlisted March 19, 1813,
Benjamin M. Parks, private, enlisted April 8, 1813,
John Parker, private, enlisted March 29, 1813,
Asa Russell, private, enlisted Feb. 10, 1813,
R. S. Robinson, private, enlisted March 27, 1813,
Josiah Richardson, private, enlisted Feb. 17, 1813,
Samuel Stevens, private, enlisted March 26, 1813,
Levi Stevens, private, enlisted March 29, 1813,
Joseph Snow, private, enlisted Feb. 12, 1813,
Franklin Spencer, private, enlisted March 18, 1813,
John Thompson, private, enlisted April 7, 1813,
James Thompson, private, enlisted March 23, 1813,
Simeon Wood, private, enlisted April 15, 1813,
Cephas White, private, enlisted April 5, 1813,
Simeon Warner, private, enlisted April 7, 1813,
William Weadon, private, enlisted March 24, 1813,
Jonathan Ward, private, enlisted March 22, 1813,

Dan Ward, private, enlisted March 22, 1813,
Omer Washburn, private, enlisted March 29, 1813,
William Warner, private, enlisted March 31, 1813,
Oliver Wright, private, enlisted April 1, 1813,
Jacob Wheeler, private, enlisted Feb. 28, 1813,
Thomas Wilcox, private, enlisted April 19, 1813.

PAYROLL OF A COMPANY OF INFANTRY COM-
MANDED BY CAPTAIN JOHN W. WEEKS, OF
THE ELEVENTH REGIMENT OF THE
UNITED STATES, FOR THE MONTHS
OF JANUARY AND FEBRUARY, 1813.

John W. Weeks, captain,
John Bliss, first lieutenant,
James Green, second lieutenant,
Daniel Bailey, sergeant,
Amaziah Knights, sergeant,
Benjamin Stephenson, sergeant,
William Smith, sergeant,
William W. Bailey, corporal,
Peter Gamsby, corporal,
Obed S. Hatch, corporal,
Josiah Reed, corporal,
Benjamin Wilson, corporal,
Allen Smith, musician,
Silas Whitney, musician,
Samuel Abbott, private,
Henry Alden, private, deserted from the Fourth Regi-
    ment April 23, 1809, and delivered himself to
    Lieutenant Green, Dec. 26, 1812,
Benjamin T. Baker, private,
Ebenezer Ball, private,
Job Barnet, private, died Jan. 12, 1813,
Daniel Bennet, private,

Zerah Bennet, private,
John Brown, private,
Chester Bunnell, private,
Hazen Burbank, private,
Daniel Burbank, private,
Stephen Bullard, private,
Zebulon Caswell, private,
Stephen Chase, private,
Levi Christian, private,
Seth Clark, private,
Philo Cobb, private, died Feb. 22, 1813,
John Collins, private,
Winthrop Collins, private,
John Cummins, private, died Dec. 15, 1812,
Jeremiah Clough, private,
Guy Clark, private,
Charles Collins, private,
Moses Cooper, private,
Eli Darling, private, deserted Jan. 1, 1813,
Phineas Davenport, private,
Eliphalet Day, private,
Oliver R. Dexter, private,
John Dunlap, private, doing duty and paid in the
    Twenty-first Regiment,
Moses Davis, private,
Eli Davenport, private,
John Dodge, private,
James French, private,
Abner Gay, private,
Wells Goodwin, private,
Samuel Henry, private,
John Holmes, private, died May 2, 1813,
Nehemiah Houghton, private,

Robert Hunkings, private,
Willard Huntoon, private,
Alpheus Hutchins, private,
James Harvey, private,
Joseph Henderson, private,
John Ingerson, private, deserted Jan. 1, 1813,
Warren Kasson, private,
James King, private, died in gaol at Amherst, N. H.
Joseph Labare, private,
Peter Labare, private,
Jacob MacIntire, private,
James Millen, private,
Harvey Moore, private,
Shepherd Morse, private,
Ebenezer Mudge, private,
Joseph Mullikin, private, deserted Jan. 1, 1813,
James Nesmith, private,
Stephen Orr, private,
Joseph Parker, private, deserted Feb. 4, 1813,
Daniel Perkins, private,
Theodore Phelps, private,
James Perkins, private,
Benoni Potter, private,
Orange Pixley, private,
Caleb Prouty, private,
Albert Rathbone, private,
Robert H. Robertson, private,
Amphony C. Redfield, private,
Edmond Sanborn, private,
John Sanford, private,
John Shirley, private,
Daniel Shirley, private, deserted Jan. 1, 1813,
Henry Smith, private, discharged Jan. 22, 1813,

Job Smith, private,
Luther Southworth, private,
Elihu Spencer, private,
Jacob Sperry, private,
George Sharland, private,
Jacob J. Trussell, private,
Samuel Vanshaick, private,
Amos Webster, private, deserted Jan. 1, 1813,
John Weeks, private, discharged Jan. 22, 1813,
Nehemiah West, private,
Jeremiah Wheeler, private,
Barney B. Whipple, private,
James Whitney, private,
Jeremiah White, private,
Ziba White, private, deserted Jan. 1, 1813,
Jotham Wilkins, private,
John Wilkinson, private,
Absalom Wilson, private,
John Wilson, private,
James Witherell, private,
John Wyatt, private,
John M. Williams, private,
Joseph Weed, private,
Allen White, private,
Andrew Woods, private.

PAYROLL OF CAPTAIN JOHN W. WEEKS' COMPANY, MAY 31, 1813.

Elisha B. Green, sergeant,
Samuel Abbott, private,
Thomas Alverson, private,
Nathaniel Bennet, private,

John Bickford, private,
John Burgin, Jr., private,
John Burnes, private,
Ebenezer Brainerd, private,
Gad Beacher, private,
John Brainard, private,
Thomas Brigham, private,
Jesse Cain, private,
Sylvanus Currier, private, confined at Haverhill, N. H.
Otis Chaffee, private,
Solomon B. Clark, private,
Charles Collins, private,
Benjamin Cross, private,
Samuel A. Craigue, private,
Moses Cooper, private,
Jeremiah Clough, private,
Zimner Dodge, private,
John Dodge, private,
John English, private,
Luther Fuller, private,
Jeremiah Fuller, private,
Calvin Fuller, private, died April 19, 1813,
Timothy Fuller, private, died May 13, 1813,
Lemuel Fuller, private,
John French, private,
Joel Farnham, private,
Robert Gothan, private,
Samuel Gothan, private,
Henry Hall, private,
John Hicks, private,
Daniel Holmes, private, died May 6, 1813,
Sheldon Holbrook, private,
Greenlief Huntoon, private,

George Huntoon, private,
George Ingersol, private, died April 13, 1813,
Joshua Knapp, private,
George W. Lucas, private,
Samuel Linsey, private
William Merriam, private,
Nathan Moores, private,
Jacob B. Moores, private, died May 16, 1813,
John W. Moores, private,
Orsmus Page, private, died April 8, 1813,
Daniel Pinkham, private,
Martin Pray, private,
Levi Pratt, private,
Abraham Rogers, private,
Abram Sanborn, private,
Joshua Stephens, private,
Israel Sanderson, private,
James P. Stanley, private,
Reuben Stephens, private,
John M. Straw, private, died March 26, 1813,
David Stoddard, private,
John C. Swain, private,
Daniel Stratton, private,
Eliphalet Taylor, private,
Daniel Utley, private,
Simeon Warner, private,
George Warren, private,
Josiah Washburn, private,
Thomas Whitton, private,
John M. Williams, private,
Andrew Woods, private.

PAYROLL OF A COMPANY OF INFANTRY, COM-
MANDED BY LIEUTENANT WILLIAM S. FOS-
TER, OF THE ELEVENTH REGIMENT OF
THE UNITED STATES, FOR THE
MONTHS OF JANUARY AND
FEBRUARY, 1813.

William S. Foster, first lieutenant,
James Wells, second lieutenant,
Ezekiel Jewett, ensign,
Joseph Hopkins, sergeant,
Adam Johnson, sergeant,
Jeremiah Kimball, sergeant,
Warren Sartwell, sergeant,
William C. Belding, corporal,
Nathaniel Black, corporal,
William Livermore, corporal,
Ebenezer Watson, fifer,
Nathaniel Bowtell, private,
Thomas Barns, private,
Timothy Barnard, private,
John Backus, private,
Daniel Ball, private,
Henry Bowtell, private,
Stephen Cummings, private,
Daniel Cary, private,

Ebenezer Carlton, private,
Samuel Danforth, private,
Stephen Davis, private,
Samuel Daniels, private,
Jones Depuin, private,
Phineas Fogg, private,
Nathan Fitch, private,
Rufus Graves, private,
Lewis Hastings, private,
James Himes, private,
John Hart, private,
Benjamin Livingston, private,
James M. Lane, private,
Hezekiah McLaughlin, private,
Daniel Mixter, private,
Peter Mason, private,
Reuben Pane, private,
Jacob Reed, private,
Samuel Rice, private,
Nathaniel Rice, private,
William Smith, private,
Thomas Spalding, private,
Peter Wiley, private,
William Wells, private,
Danford Worthington, private.

PAYROLL OF LIEUTENANT WILLIAM S. FOSTER'S COMPANY,
MAY 31, 1813.

Silas W. C. Chase, sergeant, enlisted May 10, 1813,
Abraham Fuller, sergeant, enlisted April 30, 1813,
Hubbard Cross, corporal, enlisted April 8, 1813,
Dudley Tibbits, corporal, enlisted Feb. 4, 1813,
Lathrop Wells, musician, enlisted Jan. 6, 1813,

Benjamin Beckwith, private, enlisted Jan. 28, 1813, deserted April 1, 1813,

Henry Boutwell, private, enlisted Jan. 30, 1813,

David Brown, private, enlisted Jan. 12, 1813,

John Deputnin, private, enlisted Feb. 27, 1813, died April 20, 1813,

James Deputnin, private, enlisted Jan. 1, 1813,

John C. Eastman, private, enlisted March 9, 1813, deserted April 15, 1813,

Levi Easterbrooks, private, enlisted Jan. 1, 1813,

Samuel Emerson, private, enlisted Jan. 11, 1813,

Daniel Ellis, private, enlisted Feb. 6, 1813, died April 10, 1813,

John Fisher, private, enlisted April 5, 1813,

John W. Franklin, private, enlisted Jan. 11, 1813,

Edmond Freeman, private, enlisted Jan. 11, 1813,

Joseph Fuller, private, enlisted Feb. 6, 1813,

Ebenezer Futts, private, enlisted April 2, 1813,

Moses George, private, enlisted April 7, 1813,

James Glidden, private, enlisted March 6, 1813, deserted April 16, 1813,

James Harvey, private, enlisted April 4, 1813,

Nathaniel Hunt, private, enlisted Jan. 9, 1813,

Samuel Hall, private, enlisted March 29, 1813,

Isaac Lock, private, enlisted March 18, 1813,

Daniel Lee, private, enlisted May 14, 1813,

Benjamin Morse, private, enlisted April 1, 1813,

Elisha Meads, private, enlisted March 29, 1813,

Solomon Otis, private, enlisted March 5, 1813,

Ebenezer Place, private, enlisted March 9, 1813,

Joseph Putney, private, enlisted April 1, 1813,

Joseph Plumm, private, enlisted Feb. 6, 1813,

Ambrose Renell, private, enlisted Feb. 4, 1813,

Abraham Richards, private, enlisted March 17, 1813,
James Richards, private, enlisted Feb. 5, 1813,
Jonas Richards, private, enlisted Feb. 9, 1813,
Stephen Richards, private, enlisted Jan. 20, 1813,
John Smart, private, enlisted April 1, 1813,
Benjamin Smith, private, enlisted April 2, 1813,
Isaac Smith, private, enlisted April 5, 1813,
John Smith, private, enlisted April 1, 1813,
Joseph Trufont, private, enlisted April 2, 1813,
John B. Whitehouse, private, enlisted April 14, 1813,
Moses Warner, private, enlisted Feb. 12, 1813, deserted
    Feb. 22, 1813,
Winslow Whiting, private, enlisted April 3, 1813,
Caleb Young, private, enlisted April 14, 1813.

PAYROLL OF A COMPANY OF INFANTRY COM-
MANDED BY CAPTAIN JOHN McNEIL, Jr.,
OF THE ELEVENTH REGIMENT OF THE
UNITED STATES, FOR THE MONTHS
OF JANUARY AND FEBRUARY,
1813.

John McNeil, Jr., captain,
Richard Bean, first lieutenant,
Timothy Aldrich, ensign,
Hazen Bedel, sergeant,
Thomas Dickey, sergeant,
Joseph E. Marritt, sergeant, appointed paymaster's
    assistant Jan. 25, 1813,
David Pratt, sergeant,
Abraham Doolittle, corporal,
Moses Flanders, corporal,
Henry Ferguson, corporal,
Bradley French, corporal,
Peter Hildreth, corporal,
Jesse Marshall, corporal,
Thomas Smith, musician,
David Small, musician,
Benjamin Abbott, private,
James Allard, private,
Isaac Baldwin, private,

Lotan Bartlett, private,
Thomas Bentley, private,
John Blake, private,
Joseph Burke, private,
Joseph Buss, private,
Benjamin Butcher, private,
Chester Carpenter, private,
Samuel Caswell, private,
Benjamin Clemons, private,
Joseph Chapman, private,
James Courrier, private, died Feb. 5, 1813,
Caleb Courrier, private,
Benjamin Davis, private,
Jonathan Dowe, private,
James Davis, private, died Jan. 18, 1813,
Chellis Eastman, private, died Jan. 13, 1813.
Aaron Foster, private,
Stephen Gale, private, absent without leave,
Benjamin Hall, private,
Peter Hamilton, private,
Nathaniel Hoyt, private,
James Head, Jr., private, absent without leave, never
    mustered and never paid,
Alexander Jones, private,
Sylvanus Learned, private,
Isaac Littlehale, private,
Levi Miller, private, absent without leave,
James Masters, private,
William Moody, private,
Elihu Mott, private,
Moses B. Morrison, private,
Jonathan Nichols, private,
David J. Pratt, private,

Robert Purple, private,
John Pierce, private,
Daniel Richardson, private,
Jonas Richardson, private,
Samuel Race, private,
Benjamin Roe, private,
Sterlen Sargeants, private,
John D. Small, private,
Edward Small, private,
Samuel Small, private,
Banfield Scott, private,
Zuinlins Skinner, private,
James Staples, private,
John Stanley, private,
Gideon Thomas, private,
Loren Temple, private,
Isaac Whitcomb, private,
Moses T. Willard, private.

PAYROLL OF CAPTAIN JOHN McNEIL, JR.'S, COMPANY, MAY
31, 1813.

Isaac I. Davis, sergeant,
Henry Eastman, sergeant,
Samuel Ames, private, enlisted Jan. 23, 1813,
Wells Ames, private, enlisted Jan. 23, 1813,
John Abbott, private, enlisted Feb. 3, 1813, died April 13,
    1813,
Calvin J. Aldrich, private, enlisted March 17, 1813,
Caleb Bridges, private, enlisted March 22, 1813,
Jese Case, private, enlisted Feb. 13, 1813,
Henry Dodge, private, enlisted Jan. 20, 1813,
Gordon Foster, private, enlisted March 20, 1813,
Eben Hubbard, private, enlisted Dec. 23, 1812,

Benjamin Howe, private, enlisted Jan. 23, 1813,

Joseph Hackett, private, enlisted Feb. 24, 1813,

David Learned, private, enlisted Jan. 4, 1813, deserted
      April 5, 1813,

William McKee, private, enlisted Jan. 26, 1813, died
      March 20, 1813,

Thomas Mastin, private, enlisted Jan. 11, 1813,

James Nesmith, private, enlisted Jan. 7, 1813,

Stephen Nesmith, private, enlisted Feb. 15, 1813,

John Prince, private, enlisted Feb. 13, 1813,

Billey Stearns, private, enlisted Feb. 3, 1813,

Stephen Sherman, private, enlisted Jan. 11, 1813,

Reuben Sherman, Jr., private, enlisted Jan. 19, 1813,

John Stevens, Jr., private, enlisted March 16, 1813,

Benjamin Woodbury, private, enlisted March 3, 1813,

Levi Whiteman, private, enlisted March 5, 1813.

PAYROLL OF A COMPANY OF INFANTRY COM-
MANDED BY LIEUTENANT VALENTINE R.
GOODRICH, OF THE ELEVENTH REGI-
MENT OF THE UNITED STATES,
FOR THE MONTHS OF JANUARY
AND FEBRUARY, 1813.

V. R. Goodrich, first lieutenant,
David Crawford, second lieutenant,
Thomas Levake, ensign,
William Blake, sergeant,
Stephen Howard, sergeant,
Guy Miegs, sergeant,
Zalmon C. Palmer, sergeant,
Austin Root, sergeant, died Jan. 10, 1813,
Elisha Hoyt, corporal,
Asahel Lyon, corporal,
David Moody, corporal,
Samuel M. Storey, corporal,
Russell Myrick, musician, enlisted Feb. 18, 1813,
Dwight Marsh, musician, enlisted Feb. 12, 1813,
George Algier, private,
Rufus Austin, private,
Gardener Adams, private,
Alanson Adams, private,
John J. Bissell, private,
Frederick Burnham, private,

Joseph M. Butler, private,
Timothy Burdick, private,
Orison Brink, private,
George Beals, private,
Jacob Baker, private,
James Collier, private,
Joseph Clark, private,
Amos Corey, private,
Job G. Camp, private,
Elijah Chapman, private,
Ezekiel Clough, private,
Thomas Dickinson, private,
Carey Edwards, private,
Richard Estes, private,
Ezra Eastman, private,
John Fox, private,
Amasa Follett, private,
Noel Frishet, private,
Nicholas Frimmer, private,
William Goddard, private,
Stoddard Green, private,
Stephen J. Howard, private,
Zebina Hubbard, private,
Charles Howes, private,
Timothy Hatch, private, enlisted Feb. 5, 1813, died
    April 24, 1813,
Samuel Hartley, private, enlisted Feb. 21, 1813,
Peter Jasmyn, private,
Amza Judd, private, enlisted March 1, 1813,
Cyrus Knap, private, enlisted Feb. 8, 1813,
John Lamphier, private,
Jacob Ladd, private,
Levi Lane, private, enlisted Feb. 19, 1813,

Robert Miller, private,
John Martin, private,
Peter Mosse, private,
John Myrick, private,
Lewis Marveladoo, private,
Elisha Martindale, private,
Jason Marsh, private,
William McLane, private, deserted Dec. 13, 1812,
John Neels, private,
David W. Older, private,
Cyrus Pierce, private,
Henry Perry, private,
Thomas B. Reed, private,
Levi Robinson, private,
Benjamin Stevens, private, absent without leave,
Ambrose Surrett, private,
William Sears, private,
William Thompson, private, discharged March 1,
    1813,
Gardener Wright, private,
Ephraim Wood, private,
Benjamin J. Weed, private,
Gardner Waters, private.

PAYROLL OF LIEUTENANT GOODRICH'S COMPANY, MAY 31,
                1813.

Zera Green, corporal, enlisted Jan. 21, 1813,
John Shutlock, corporal, enlisted Feb. 15, 1813,
Simon Allard, private, enlisted May 2, 1813,
Daniel Bland, private, enlisted Jan. 19, 1813,
John Bailey, private, enlisted Jan. 18, 1813, died April 6,
    1813,

John Brown, private, enlisted Jan. 1, 1813,
Wilder Brown, private, enlisted Jan. 13, 1813,
Samuel Boynton, private, enlisted Feb. 17, 1813,
Ephraim Brown, private, enlisted March 3, 1813,
David Butler, private, enlisted March 22, 1813,
Phineas E. Baion, private, enlisted Feb. 17, 1813,
John Clute, private, enlisted Feb. 12, 1813,
Henry Carpenter, private, enlisted Feb. 4, 1813,
John Colfax, private, enlisted Feb. 8, 1813,
Robert Cockle, private, enlisted March 12, 1813,
Joseph Dunking, private, enlisted Feb. 22, 1813,
Abel Davenport, private, enlisted Feb. 15, 1813,
Oliver Davis, Jr., private, enlisted Feb. 26, 1813,
Asahel Davison, private, enlisted March 5, 1813, died
    April 2, 1813,
Abner Davis, private, enlisted March 10, 1813,
Daniel Farwell, private, enlisted March 20, 1813,
Samuel Foster, private, enlisted Feb. 20, 1813,
Alexander G. Gregory, private, enlisted March 22, 1813,
Joseph Grandue, private, enlisted Feb. 18, 1813,
Francis Grandue, private, enlisted Feb. 18, 1813,
George Hyde, private, enlisted March 6, 1813,
Timothy B. Henderson, private, enlisted Feb. 5, 1813,
Martin Hatch, private, enlisted March 18, 1813,
Arleban Hatch, private, enlisted March 11, 1813,
David Martin, private, enlisted March 30, 1813,
Freeman Magee, private, enlisted March 1, 1813,
Jason Marsh, private, enlisted Feb. 12, 1813,
James McKnight, private, enlisted Feb. 27, 1813,
James McKnight, Jr., private, enlisted Feb. 27, 1813,
David McKnight, private, enlisted Feb. 27, 1813,
David Moody, private, enlisted Feb. 11, 1813,
Asa Nainamore, private, enlisted April 1, 1813,

Nathan Nay, private, enlisted March 11, 1813,
Alpheus Paul, private, enlisted March 22, 1813,
Nael Potter, private, enlisted Feb. 8, 1813,
Henry Perry, private, enlisted Feb. 10, 1813,
Reuben Phillips, private, enlisted Feb. 12, 1813,
Lawrence Pano, private, enlisted March 4, 1813,
Daniel Richardson, private, enlisted March 17, 1813,
William Reed, private, enlisted March 11, 1813,
Francis Rock, private, enlisted Feb. 8, 1813,
Levi Robinson, private, enlisted Feb. 17, died March 12,
    1813,
Abel Steele, private, enlisted Jan. 13, 1813,
Nathan Sears, private, enlisted Feb. 19, 1813,
William Sears, private, enlisted Feb. 19, 1813,
Jotham Stebbins, private, enlisted Feb. 25, 1813,
Abel Stearns, private, enlisted March 3, 1813,
William Towne, private, enlisted March 15, 1813,
Edward Taylor, private, enlisted March 10, 1813,
Simon Thrasher, private, enlisted March 8, 1813,
Ebenezer H. Wise, private, enlisted March 31, 1813,
John Wood, Jr., private, enlisted March 12, 1813,
Elias Witherbee, private, enlisted March 2, 1813,
Abiather Witherell, private, enlisted March 17, 1813,
Lewis Ward, private, enlisted Feb. 26, 1813,
Salem Wheelock, private, enlisted Feb. 21, 1813,
James Weed, private, enlisted Feb. 6, 1813,
Salmon Whitlock, private, enlisted Feb. 6, 1813,
Benjamin Weab, Jr., private, enlisted Feb. 18, 1813,
Abram Woodenbury, private, enlisted March 9, 1813.

PAYROLL OF A COMPANY OF INFANTRY COM-
MANDED BY CAPTAIN PHINEAS WILLIAMS,
OF THE ELEVENTH REGIMENT OF THE
UNITED STATES, FOR THE MONTHS
OF JANUARY AND FEBRUARY, 1813.

Phineas Williams, captain,
Malaki Corning, first lieutenant,
Abel Farwell, second lieutenant,
Newman Clarke, ensign,
Godfrey H. Belding, sergeant,
Elihu Emmons, sergeant,
Rufus T. Lillie, sergeant,
Henry Miner, sergeant,
Benjamin Putnam, sergeant,
Josiah Clark, corporal,
Benjamin Childs, corporal,
William Humphrey, corporal,
Bela Sprague, corporal,
Henry S. Wait, corporal,
Dexter Dimmock, musician,
Aaron Gardner, musician,
Daniel Bagley, private,
Henry Bentley, private,
Richard Boyington, private,
Alfred Barrell, private,

George Bean, private,
Thomas Clark, private, absent without leave,
John Clark, private,
John Cummins, private,
Reuben Clough, private,
William Courrier, private,
Aaron Crandall, private,
Peter Darling, private, absent without leave,
George Fuller, private,
Wilson Fisher, private,
Reuben Fuller, private,
Nathaniel Gould, private,
Oliver Galusha, private,
Peter Goodrich, private,
William Harvey, private,
Charles C. Holcomb, private, died Dec. 10, 1812,
Elisha Hardy, private,
Ira Houghton, private, deserted Sept. 6, 1812, gave
    himself up Sept. 11, 1812,
Seth Ingraham, private,
Luke Lamphier, private, discharged Feb. 7, 1813,
Charles Lamphier, private,
Eliphalet Maxfield, private,
John McLeod, private,
Samuel Miller, private,
William S. Messenger, private,
Joseph Paterson, private,
Thomas Perkins, private,
Benjamin Runolds, private,
Ebenezer Rogers, private,
Hosea Remington, private,
Jonathan Remington, private,
Robert Wright, private.

PAYROLL OF CAPTAIN PHINEAS WILLIAMS' COMPANY, MAY 31, 1813.

Ira Butler, private, enlisted March 17, 1813,
Paul Brewster, private, enlisted March 22, 1813,
Timothy Bradford, private, enlisted March 23, 1813,
Job Barnett, private, enlisted Jan. 29, 1813,
William Cheny, private, enlisted March 3, 1813,
William R. Call, private, enlisted March 18, 1813,
Isaac Churchill, private, enlisted March 27, 1813,
Joseph Dodge, private, enlisted March 15, 1813,
Abner Eaton, private, enlisted Jan. 9, 1813,
Joel Greely, private, enlisted Jan. 29, 1813,
John Gubliat, private, enlisted March 26, 1813,
Abbot Gould, private, enlisted Feb. 1, 1813,
Asa Hopkins, private, enlisted March 13, 1813,
Israel Houghton, private, enlisted Feb. 12, 1813,
John Johnson, private, enlisted March 29, 1813,
Abraham Jackson, private, enlisted Jan. 27, 1813,
Asa Kenney, private, enlisted Feb. 15, 1813,
Barnabas Keth, private, enlisted Feb. 20, 1813,
Shubael Lamphier, private, enlisted Feb. 2, 1813,
Zebina Logan, private, enlisted Feb. 12, 1813,
William Lacouse, private, enlisted August 14, 1812,
Roswell Lamphier, private, enlisted Dec. 22, 1812,
Levi Maxfield, private, enlisted March 26, 1813,
Ethany Miller, private, enlisted March 5, 1813,
Moses McFarson, private, enlisted Jan. 27, 1813,
Benjamin Ordeway, private, enlisted Jan. 14, 1813,
Abizer Perkins, private, enlisted March 20, 1813,
John Perkins, Jr., private, enlisted March 5, 1813, died
    April 24, 1813,
Oliver Plaisted, private, enlisted Feb. 20, 1813, died April
    4, 1813,

William Plaisted, private, enlisted Feb. 13, 1813,
John Procter, private, enlisted April 23, 1813,
Jonathan C. Parker, private, enlisted March 3, 1813,
Elijah Packard, private, enlisted March 26, 1813,
James Rich, private, enlisted April 13, 1813,
Martin Rogers, private, enlisted March 19, 1813,
Warren Ransom, private, enlisted March 3, 1813,
Isaac Spooner, private, enlisted Feb. 12, 1813,
James Tarble, private, enlisted Feb. 13, 1813,
William Voughn, private, enlisted Feb. 20, 1813,
William West, private, enlisted Feb. 10, 1813,
Nathan West, private, enlisted Feb. 20, 1813,
David White, private, enlisted Feb. 28, 1813,
Benjamin White, private, enlisted Feb. 28, 1813,
Caleb Willard, private, enlisted Feb. 2, 1813.

PAYROLL OF A DETACHMENT OF RECRUITS
UNDER THE COMMAND OF CAPTAIN JONA-
THAN STARKS, OF THE ELEVENTH
REGIMENT OF UNITED STATES
INFANTRY, MAY 31, 1813.

Matthias Avery, private, enlisted March 20, 1813,
Shederah Avery, private, enlisted March 10, 1813,
Jacob Avery, private, enlisted March 8, 1813,
Henry Allard, private, enlisted March 22, 1813,
Josiah Bridges, private, enlisted Jan. 14, 1813,
Josiah Burgess, private, enlisted Feb. 27, 1813, deserted
    March 4, 1813,
Isaac Bickford, private, enlisted Jan. 8, 1813,
Enoch Colby, private, enlisted Feb. 8, 1813, deserted Feb.
    15, 1813,
Nathaniel Cook, private, enlisted Jan. 9, 1813, died April
    25, 1813,
Daniel Collins, private, deserted Feb. 10, 1813,
Nathaniel Cook, Jr., private, enlisted Jan. 11, 1813,
James Cook, private, enlisted March 28, 1813,
Caleb Downing, private, enlisted Feb. 11, 1813, deserted
    April 14, 1813,
Moses Drown, private, enlisted Jan. 13, 1813,
Samuel Drown, private, enlisted Jan. 1, 1813,

Solomon Davis, private, enlisted April 3, 1813,
Thomas Drew, private, enlisted Jan. 6, 1813,
Moses Fall, private, enlisted Feb. 12, 1813,
John Glines, private, enlisted March 5, 1813,
James Goodwin, private, enlisted Feb. 12, 1813,
John Gilman, private, enlisted Feb. 20, 1813,
William Healey, private, enlisted Feb. 10, 1813,
Joseph Ham, private, enlisted Jan. 30, 1813,
Nicholas Hodgedon, private, enlisted Jan. 2, 1813, de-
     serted March 5, 1813,
John Hunt, private, enlisted March 20, 1813, captured
     June 3, 1813, on Lake Champlain,
Jonathan Kennison, private, enlisted March 11, 1813,
John Kennison, private, enlisted March 1, 1813,
Pardon W. Keene, private, enlisted April 3, 1813,
Steven Maxell, private, enlisted Feb. 16, 1813,
Caleb Marstin, private, enlisted Feb. 25, 1813,
Moses Maxfield, private, enlisted Feb. 10, 1813,
David Patch, private, enlisted March 16, 1813,
John Perkins, private, enlisted March 6, 1813,
Jonathan Prince, private, enlisted March 3, 1813,
Nathaniel Palmer, private, enlisted Jan. 9, 1813,
Simeon Pearl, private, enlisted Dec. 29, 1812,
Steven Quimby, private, enlisted Feb. 8, 1813,
James Rix, private, enlisted Jan. 18, 1813, died May 8, 1813,
David Rumery, private, enlisted Jan. 4, 1813,
Benjamin Seavey, private, enlisted Feb. 29, 1813,
Hiram Stevens, private, enlisted March 9, 1813,
Samuel Stanley, private, enlisted Feb. 6, 1813,
Thomas Wedgewood, private, enlisted Feb. 20, 1813,
Robert Willey, private, enlisted Feb. 19, 1813, deserted
     March 3, 1813,
Steven Whipple, private, enlisted March 4, 1813.

PAYROLL OF CAPTAIN ASAHEL SCOVELL'S COMPANY OF VOLUNTEER RIFLE CORPS, NOVEMBER 17, 1813.

Asahel Scovell, captain,
Barnard Ketcham, first lieutenant,
Philip Smith, second lieutenant,
Barnabas Myrick, cornet,
Josiah Bascomb, sergeant,
William Corey, sergeant,
James Flagg, sergeant,
Jehiel Gates, sergeant,
Dyer Bottum, corporal,
Henry G. Green, corporal,
Benjamin Knotton, corporal,
Justus Wright, corporal,
Henry Selilck, musician,
John Avory, private, horse and equipage taken by the
    enemy,
Alva Allen, private,
Benjamin Brastead, private,
Benjamin Bissell, private,
Jonas Bridge, private,
James Baker, private,
Silas Brookins, Jr., private, horse and equipage taken
    by the enemy,
Stewart Chellis, private,

Wait Chatterton, private,
Alvah Churchill, private,
Dorus Churchill, private,
David Demerry, private,
Jacob Dayton, private,
Levi Dart, private,
Spencer Doughty, private,
James Ferres, private,
Abel Griswold, private,
Anson Griswold, private,
John Gibson, Jr., private,
Asaph Griswold, private,
Gross Gates, private,
Jacob Graves, private,
Benjamin Hale, private,
David Johnson, private,
Isaac Ketchum, private,
Edward Leister, private,
Simon Lewis, private,
Nathan Myrick, private,
Joseph Mason, private,
Isaac Miller, private,
Manus Murray, private,
Eber Murray, private,
John Nobles, private,
Horatio Parks, private,
Joseph Phelps, Jr., private,
Abiel Richardson, private,
Holsey B. Scovell, private,
Samuel Shephard, private,
Hyde Westover, private, horse wounded and died on
    the march,
Alanson White, private.

PAYROLL OF A COMPANY OF ARTIFICERS, COMMANDED BY ALEXANDER PARRIS, SUPERINTENDENT OF THE CORPS OF ARTIFICERS OF THE UNITED STATES, FOR THE MONTHS OF MAY AND JUNE, 1814.

Ira Floyd, assistant superintendent,
Obed Wright, assistant superintendent,
Joseph Dunn, master,
Joseph R. Bronsdon, master carpenter,
Nathaniel Chase, master carpenter, discharged June
  1, 1814,
Cyrus Cobb, master mechanic,
Timothy Follenbee, ship carpenter,
Enus Gragg, ship carpenter,
Samuel N. Andress, carpenter,
Zebina Billings, carpenter, discharged May 22, 1813,
Stephen Bush, carpenter, discharged May 26, 1814,
Jesse Campfield, carpenter,
Thomas Clinton, carpenter, discharged June 1, 1814,
Zachariah Damon, carpenter,
John Herndon, carpenter,
David Hartshorn, carpenter,
Elisha W. Howland, carpenter,
George Lane, carpenter,

John Martin, carpenter,
Jacob Noyes, carpenter,
Christopher Phillips, ship carpenter,
John Pierce, carpenter, discharged July 11, 1814,
Charles Pinkham, carpenter, discharged June 1, 1814,
James Parker, carpenter,
Edward Richardson, carpenter,
Galen Root, carpenter,
William N. Smith, carpenter,
Timothy Sullivan, carpenter, discharged June 12,
    1814,
Fred A. Sprague, carpenter,
Moses Thomas, carpenter, discharged June 1, 1814,
Edward Thomas, carpenter,
John Wilkinson, carpenter,
Richard Waldron, carpenter,
Ebenezer Williams, carpenter, discharged June 5,
    1814,
Joseph Emery, boat builder,
James Taggert, boat builder,
Jacob Waterhouse, master blacksmith,
Elias Buck, blacksmith, discharged June 1, 1814,
Justis Pudney, blacksmith, discharged June 1, 1814,
Henry B. Callender, saddler,
Joshua Dunn, saddler,
Sterling T. Millikin, saddler,
Edward Payson, saddler, discharged June 1, 1814,
John C. Siniler, saddler,
Josiah Whitney, saddler, discharged June 1, 1814,
Jacob Eaton, armourer,
Jacob Houtzell, armourer,
Josiah Nichols, armourer,
Martin Sturtivant, armourer, discharged June 1, 1814.

Edmund Bemont, laborer, discharged June 1, 1814,
Samuel Crapon, laborer,
Asa Dibble, laborer,
William Eaton, laborer,
Ward Hatch, laborer,
Daniel Hearn, laborer,
Isaac Josselyn, laborer, discharged June 1, 1814,
Charles Page, laborer, discharged June 1, 1814,
Stephen Storrs, laborer,
Samuel E. Whicher, laborer,
William Whicher, laborer,
John Baptist, black,
Abraham Derbey, black,
Samuel Hatford, black,
Nathaniel Lawrence, black,
James Millikin, black,
Cornelius Melona, black,
Samuel W. Marshall, black,
Samuel Ridgway, black,
Nathaniel Sawyer, black,
Robert Thomas, black,
Jonathan Townsend, black,
Ebenezer Wiman, black,
Ezra Wheelock, black.

MUSTER ROLL OF A DETACHMENT IN THE REGIMENT OF UNITED STATES DRAGOONS, COMMANDED BY COLONEL JAMES BEAN, JUNE 30, 1814.

James V. Ball, major and brevet lieutenant-colonel, enlisted Sept. 16, 1812,

George Haig, captain, enlisted Jan. 20, 1813,

Clinton Wright, second lieutenant, enlisted April 19, 1814,

John L. Elbert, third lieutenant, enlisted June 20, 1813,

John Caldwell, cornet, enlisted March 11, 1814,

Aquilla Brown, sergeant, enlisted April 11, 1812, to April 10, 1817,

Samuel Chatterton, sergeant, enlisted June 1, 1812, to May 31, 1817, promoted to third lieutenant in the Forty-Eighth Regiment Infantry,

James Fly, sergeant, enlisted Jan. 5, 1813, to Jan. 4, 1818,

Harvey Graham, sergeant, enlisted April 18, 1812, to April 17, 1817,

Gilbert Hankings, sergeant, enlisted Dec. 24, 1812, to June 23, 1814, prisoner of war,

William Lookadoo, sergeant, enlisted May 2, 1812, to May 1, 1817,

William Layer, sergeant, enlisted May 18, 1812, to May 17, 1817,

Richard Scott, sergeant, enlisted Sept. 9, 1812, to Sept. 8, 1817, on command on Lake Champlain,

Joseph Wheeler, sergeant, enlisted June 19, 1812, to June 18, 1817,

Jesse Whitaker, sergeant, enlisted May 25, 1812, to May 24, 1817,

Simon Brown, corporal, enlisted June 28, 1812, to June 27, 1817,

Isaac Blanchard, corporal, enlisted Feb. 25, 1813, to Feb. 24, 1818,

Nicholas Duclos, corporal, enlisted Feb. 14, 1813, to Feb. 13, 1818,

Chauncey W. Fuller, corporal, enlisted June 15, 1812, to June 14, 1817,

Nathan B. Harvey, corporal, enlisted Feb. 25, 1813, to Feb. 24, 1818,

Bernard Miller, corporal, enlisted Oct. 9, 1812, to Oct. 8, 1817;

Bartlet Nash, corporal, prisoner of war, wounded, unfit for service,

Robert Titas, corporal, enlisted June 30, 1812, to June 29, 1817,

James Webber, corporal, enlisted Jan. 5, 1813, to Jan. 4, 1818,

Alvin Bugbee, trumpeter, enlisted Jan. 24, 1813, to Jan. 23, 1818,

Jesse Ferguson, trumpeter, enlisted Sept. 20, 1812, to Sept. 19, 1817,

Milton Race, trumpeter, enlisted June 17, 1812, to June 16, 1817,

Offin Barrett, saddler, enlisted March 2, 1813, to Sept. 1, 1814,

John Camp, saddler, enlisted July 6, 1812, to July 5, 1817,

Simon S. Morrill, blacksmith, enlisted Aug. 24, 1812, to Aug. 23, 1817,

John Powers, blacksmith, enlisted Feb. 18, 1813, to Feb. 17, 1818,

Edward Wilcox, farrier, enlisted Sept. 5, 1812, to Sept. 4, 1817,

Edward Abel, private, enlisted Sept. 8, 1812, to Sept. 7, 1817,

Joshua Ash, private, enlisted June 17, 1812, to June 16, 1817,

Samuel Adams, private, prisoner of war,

Roswell Bates, private, enlisted May 30, 1812, to May 29, 1817,

Marcus Beacher, private, enlisted May 28, 1812, to May 17, 1817,

Isaac Baker, private, enlisted Oct. 11, 1812, to Oct. 10, 1817,

Peter Bartholomew, private, enlisted Oct. 9, 1812, to Oct. 8, 1817,

Joshua Bussell, private, enlisted Jan. 5, 1813, to Jan. 4, 1818, wounded at Chazy,

Thomas Cox, private, enlisted March 13, 1812, to March 12, 1817,

James Carlisle, private, enlisted Oct. 2, 1812, to April 1, 1814,

Thomas A. Clark, private, enlisted Jan. 31, 1813, to Jan. 30, 1818,

John W. Creamer, private, enlisted Sept. 4, 1812, deserted,

William Clare, private, prisoner of war,

Michael Colbough, private, prisoner of war,

Thomas C. Douty, private, enlisted Feb. 5, 1813, to Feb. 4, 1818,

William Eldridge, private, enlisted June 21, 1812, to June 20, 1817,

Jonathan Elkins, private, enlisted May 19, 1812, to May 18, 1817,

Thomas Eddy, prisoner of war,

Hayes Falkenburg, private, enlisted Aug. 12, 1812, to Aug. 11, 1817,

Daniel Frazier, private, enlisted March 10, 1813, to March 9, 1818,

Abraham Grumendike, private, enlisted Oct. 9, 1812, to Oct. 8, 1817,

Daniel B. Gill, private, enlisted June 24, 1812, to June 23, 1817,

Ephraim Hartshorn, private, enlisted Dec. 28, 1812, to Dec. 21, 1817,

Elbridge G. Hemenway, private, enlisted Feb. 10, 1813, to Feb. 9, 1818,

Stephen F. Hemenway, private, enlisted May 27, 1812, to May 26, 1817,

Samuel Haviland, private, enlisted Jan. 1, 1813, to Dec. 31, 1817,

John Hyde, private, enlisted June 2, 1812, to June 1, 1817, waiter in hospital in Burlington,

Thomas Harvey, private, enlisted Feb. 26, 1812, to Feb. 26, 1817,

Alvin Hieght, private, enlisted Jan. 8, 1812, to Jan. 7, 1817,

Luke Holbrook, private, enlisted Feb. 26, 1812, to Feb. 25, 1817,

Philip Henning, private, enlisted Feb. 23, 1812, to Feb. 22, 1819,

John Heath, private, prisoner of war,

Edward Howard, private, prisoner of war,

Jacob Hymer, private, prisoner of war,

John Johnson, private, enlisted Feb. 25, 1814, to Feb. 24, 1819,

Ebenezer King, private, enlisted April 1, 1813, to March 31, 1818,

Abel Kimball, private, prisoner of war,

James Landon, private, enlisted Sept. 3, 1812, to Sept. 2, 1817,

Henry Laflin, private, enlisted April 14, 1813, to April 13, 1818,

Joseph Lochlin, private, enlisted June 18, 1812, to June 17, 1817,

Otis Ladd, private, enlisted June 15, 1812, to June 14, 1817,

James Lucas, private, enlisted June 27, 1812, to June 26, 1817,

George Lathrop, private, enlisted May 23, 1812, to May 22, 1817,

Solomon Langmaid, private, enlisted Jan. 14, 1813, to Jan. 13, 1818,

William Lyons, private, enlisted Oct. 9, 1812, to Oct. 8, 1817,

Ashley Millard, private, enlisted June 21, 1812, to June 26, 1817,

Seth Miller, private, enlisted June 3, 1812, to June 2, 1817,

Milo McIntosh, private, enlisted June 19, 1812, to June 18, 1817,

James McAllister, private, enlisted July 6, 1812, to July 5, 1817,

John Mudget, private, enlisted June 28, 1812, deserted,

Oliver Morris, private, enlisted June 25, 1812, to June 24, 1817,

William Matthews, private, enlisted Aug. 25, 1812, to Aug. 24, 1817,

William C. McDonough, private, enlisted Oct. 18, 1812, to Oct. 17, 1817,

Alexander McGee, private, enlisted Sept. 10, 1812, to Sept. 9, 1817,

Jason Metcalf, private, enlisted Feb. 20, 1813, to Feb. 19, 1818,

Samuel A. Miller, private, enlisted June 15, 1812, to June 14, 1817,

Silas W. Moses, private, enlisted Feb. 25, 1813, to Feb. 24, 1818, under sentence of general court martial,

Samuel B. Mealy, private, enlisted Feb. 23, 1814,

Daniel Otis, private, enlisted Jan. 4, 1813, to Jan. 3, 1818,

Gerrish Pulsifer, private, enlisted Feb. 18, 1813, to Feb. 17, 1818,

Raymond Quinn, private, prisoner of war,

Dennison R. Rose, private, enlisted June 15, 1812, to June 14, 1817, sick in Burlington,

Daniel Ring, private, enlisted Jan. 7, 1813, to Jan. 6, 1818,

Chace Robinson, private, enlisted Jan. 7, 1813, to Jan. 6, 1818,

Benjamin Russon, private, enlisted July 24, 1813, to July 23, 1818,

Lyman Reynolds, private, enlisted Feb. 24, 1813, to Feb. 23, 1818,

Ebenezer Richardson, private, enlisted Sept. 9, 1812, to Sept. 8, 1817,

John Rawlins, private, enlisted Jan. 5, 1813, to Jan. 4, 1818,

George R. Snyder, private, enlisted Sept. 29, 1812, to Sept. 28, 1817,

Thomas Sanderson, private, enlisted Jan. 17, 1812, to Jan. 16, 1817,

Benjamin Smith, private, enlisted Jan. 31, 1813, to Jan. 30, 1818,

David Staples, private, enlisted Feb. 18, 1813, to Feb. 17, 1818,

Charles Shaw, private, enlisted July 6, 1812, to July 5, 1817,

Henry L. Shoff, private, enlisted May 29, 1812, to May 28, 1817,

James N. Smith, private, enlisted July 29, 1812, to July 23, 1817,

John Shoot, private, prisoner of war,

James Sprott, private, prisoner of war,

David Tilton, private, enlisted May 28, 1812, to May 27, 1817,

Obediah Taylor, private, enlisted March 26, 1813, to March 25, 1818,

Nathan Thorpe, private, enlisted Oct. 3, 1812, to Oct. 7, 1817,

Ralph Tucker, private, enlisted Sept. 13, 1812, to Sept. 12, 1817,

Charles Tole, private, enlisted August 5, 1812, to August 5, 1817,

Dow Therber, private, prisoner of war,

Jeremiah Walker, private, enlisted Jan. 5, 1813, to Jan. 4, 1818,

Walter Waller, private, enlisted Feb. 10, 1813, to Feb. 9, 1818,

James Watson, private, enlisted Jan. 5, 1813, deserted,

Lyman Wheeler, private, enlisted March 2, 1813, to March 1, 1818,

Daniel Wilson, private, enlisted June 3, 1812, to June 2, 1817,
John Wilson, private, enlisted March 21, 1813, to March 23,
    1818,
Jabez Waldron, private, enlisted Dec. 12, 1812, to Dec. 11,
    1817,
John Wentworth, private, enlisted Jan. 12, 1813, to Jan. 11,
    1818,
Edward, waiter,
Henry, waiter,
Isaac, waiter,
Moses, waiter.

MUSTER ROLL OF THE LATE CAPTAIN J. BROOKS' COMPANY, COMMANDED BY LIEUTENANT JOHN J. CROMWELL, IN THE CORPS OF UNITED STATES ARTILLERY, JUNE 30, 1814.

Jonathan Brooks, captain,

John Montfort, first lieutenant, enlisted June 6, 1814,

John J. Cromwell, second lieutenant, enlisted Nov. 3, 1812, appointed conductor of artillery May 12, 1814,

Francis P. Woolsey, second lieutenant, enlisted May 20, 1813, transferred to Captain A. S. Brooks' Company,

Samuel C. Wright, clerk, enlisted Nov. 2, 1812, appointed clerk to the district pay master at Burlington, May 1, 1814,

Richard Ambrose, sergeant, enlisted June 2, 1812,

John Burr, sergeant, enlisted Nov. 21, 1812,

Jeremiah Barton, sergeant, enlisted April 11, 1813,

Zacariah Lewis, sergeant, enlisted Nov. 18, 1812,

Benjamin Smedes, sergeant, enlisted Feb. 1, 1813, promoted from corporal June 1, 1814,

Levven Spriggs, sergeant, prisoner of war on parole, transferred from Captain Leonard's Company by order of General Macomb,

Jonathan Vandegrift, sergeant, enlisted Nov. 16, 1812,

Reuben Wells, sergeant, enlisted Feb. 25, 1814, transferred from Captain Collins' Company by order of General Macomb,

Samuel Andrews, corporal, prisoner of war on parole,

Thomas Brown, corporal, enlisted May 2, 1814, promoted
from private June 1, 1814,

Daniel Gover, corporal, enlisted Feb. 22, 1813,

David Hall, corporal, enlisted Feb. 1, 1813, promoted
from private May 1, 1814,

William Martin, corporal, enlisted Oct. 22, 1812, deserted,

John McMannus, corporal, prisoner of war on parole,

Franklin Root, corporal, enlisted May 7, 1813, promoted
from private May 1, 1814,

Daniel Tingley, corporal, enlisted Oct. 28, 1812,

Philip S. Vanankin, corporal, enlisted Oct. 24, 1812,

Jacob Bainey, musician, enlisted Jan. 17, 1814, transferred from Captain Collins' Company by order of
General Macomb,

James Cole, musician, prisoner of war on parole,

David Chadwick, musician, enlisted March 10, 1813,
transferred from Captain Leonard's Company by
order of General Macomb,

Seth Goff, musician, enlisted May 7, 1813,

Elias Shepherd, musician, prisoner of war on parole,
transferred from Captain Leonard's Company by
order of General Macomb,

Ira C. Allen, artificer, enlisted July 27, 1812,

Benjamin Jenkins, artificer, enlisted Aug. 6, 1813,

Samuel Lee, artificer, enlisted March 24, 1813,

Nathan Stone, artificer, enlisted June 10, 1812,

David Allen, private, enlisted Dec. 19, 1812,

Samuel Allen, private, enlisted June 15, 1813,

Elijah Ayers, private, enlisted June 18, 1812,

Joseph Ayers, private, enlisted March 27, 1813,

James Anderson, private, enlisted July 25, 1813,

David Aldridge, private, enlisted Jan. 10, 1814,

James Brower, private, enlisted Nov. 6, 1812,
John Bickley, private, enlisted Dec. 25, 1812,
Paul Brewett, private, enlisted June 3, 1812,
Joseph O. Barton, private, enlisted Dec. 20, 1813,
Cornelius Boremus, private, enlisted Dec. 1, 1812,
Jonathan Billings, private, prisoner of war on parole,
    transferred from Captain Leonard's Company by
    order of General Macomb,
William Barney, private, enlisted Dec. 7, 1813, trans-
    ferred from Captain Collins' Company by order of
    General Macomb,
William Cook, private waiter to Lieutenant Cromwell,
Daniel Conklin, private, enlisted March 11, 1813,
John Capps, private, enlisted March 14, 1813,
John Chase, private, enlisted March 25, 1813,
Elijah Collins, private, enlisted Dec. 23, 1813, trans-
    ferred from Captain Leonard's Company by order
    of General Macomb,
William Curley, private, prisoner of war on parole,
Joseph L. Calder, private, enlisted Feb. 16, 1814, trans-
    ferred from Captain Collins' Company by order of
    General Macomb,
Josiah Dunham, private, enlisted March 4, 1813,
Isaac Dempsey, private, enlisted April 5, 1813,
John Dingley, private, enlisted Sept. 24, 1813,
Philip Demear, private, enlisted Sept. 9, 1813,
Adam Day, private, enlisted April 25, 1813,
Samuel Ellis, private, enlisted Oct. 22, 1812,
John Edwards, private, enlisted Feb. 1, 1813,
Edward Emmery, private, enlisted June 27, 1812,
Daniel Fletcher, private, enlisted March 20, 1813,
Samuel D. Freleigh, private, enlisted July 1, 1812,
Edward Fitzpatrick, private, prisoner of war on parole,

deserted from Plattsburgh, transferred from Captain
Leonard's Company by order of General Macomb,
John Flemming, private, enlisted May 4, 1814, prisoner
of war, whose term of service had expired,
Henry Finch, private, prisoner of war on parole, trans-
ferred from Captain Leonard's Company by order
of General Macomb,
Daniel S. George, private, enlisted April 15, 1813,
Isaac Grim, private, enlisted July 27, 1813,
Francis Gillett, private, enlisted, July 20, 1812,
Henry Green, private, enlisted Oct. 8, 1813, boy learn-
ing music, transferred from Captain Collins' Com-
pany,
Samuel A. Glynn, private, enlisted March 10, 1814,
Joseph Goellet, private, enlisted June 14, 1814,
William Hadden, private, enlisted Nov. 21, 1812,
Cornelius Hendrickson, private, enlisted Dec. 16, 1812,
Sylvanus Hicks, private, enlisted June 12, 1813,
William Hennesy, private, enlisted Feb. 11, 1813,
David Hannaford, private, enlisted April 24, 1813,
Charles Holmes, private, prisoner of war on parole,
transferred from Captain Leonard's Company by
order of General Izard,
Gideon Johnston, private, enlisted Nov. 6, 1812,
Hiram Jones, private, enlisted March 25, 1813, on
command with Lieutenant Spencer, assistant deputy
quartermaster-general, by order of Captain Brooks,
William Jackson, private, enlisted Feb. 20, 1814,
John Lent, private, enlisted Dec. 1, 1812,
Elijah Lee, private, enlisted Dec. 24, 1812,
Isaac Long, private, enlisted June 9, 1813,
Nathaniel Loomis, private, enlisted Feb. 22, 1813,
James Lake, private, enlisted August 6, 1813,

William Miller, private, enlisted Dec. 9, 1812,
Charles Mooney, private, enlisted June 15, 1813,
David Morgan, private, enlisted April 7, 1813,
Francis Mosso, private, enlisted March 23, 1813,
Joseph Montey, private, enlisted Feb. 12, 1814,
Abraham Montey, private, enlisted Feb. 14, 1814,
William Morrisson, private, prisoner of war on parole,
Benjamin Marker, private, prisoner of war on parole,
James McCoy, private, enlisted Feb. 16, 1814,
John Moulton, private, enlisted May 11, 1812, deserted
  from Captain Watson's Company, Sept. 20, 1812,
  and returned to duty June 28, 1814, to make good
  one year, nine months, and eight days lost by
  desertion. Transferred to the Twenty-second
  Regiment Infantry by order of the Inspector-
  General. Infantry Clerk to Brigade-Major Duncan,
Warren Nichols, private, enlisted May 28, 1813,
Jonathan Nunn, private, prisoner of war on parole,
  transferred from Captain Leonard's Company by
  order of General Izard,
Samuel Ogden, private, enlisted Nov. 11, 1812,
John Oudercarrick, private, enlisted July 5, 1813,
Jeremiah Patterson, private, enlisted Oct. 28, 1812,
Isaac Parcels, private, enlisted Dec. 4, 1812,
Amos Parker, private, enlisted Sept. 19, 1812, boy
  learning music,
Ichabod Parmenter, private, enlisted Jan. 1, 1813, reën-
  listed June 3, 1814,
Francis Platt, private, enlisted July 11, 1812,
John Pero, private, enlisted Jan. 8, 1814,
William Ryno, private, enlisted Nov. 25, 1812,
Joseph Rasco, private, enlisted Dec. 1, 1812,

William Roll, private, enlisted Jan. 6, 1813, died at
    Plattsburgh, N. Y., June 13, 1814,
John Ring, private, enlisted May 1, 1813,
Seth Richardson, private, enlisted April 6, 1813, deserted
    from Plattsburgh June 3, 1813,
Silas Raymond, private, enlisted June 22, 1812,
Sylvester Rowney, private, enlisted May 10, 1813,
Thomas Reading, private, prisoner of war on parole,
    transferred from Captain Leonard's Company by
    order of General Macomb,
Joseph Stalter, private, enlisted Nov. 2, 1812,
Pember W. Still, private, enlisted Dec. 11, 1813,
John F. W. Stone, private, prisoner of war on parole,
Joseph Sheffield, private, prisoner of war on parole,
    transferred from Captain Leonard's Company by
    order of General Macomb,
Eleazer Seevy, private, enlisted May 10, 1813,
Benjamin Smith, private, enlisted March 2, 1813,
Obediah Spencer, private, enlisted June 14, 1813,
    deserted May 18, 1814, from the general hospital
    at Plattsburgh, N. Y.,
Lemuel Thomas, private, enlisted July 4, 1812,
Allen Thomas, private, prisoner of war on parole,
John Thompson, private, enlisted Sept. 28, 1813, trans-
    ferred from Captain Collins' Company by order of
    General Macomb,
Solomon Tinsler, private, enlisted March 2, 1814, trans-
    ferred from Captain Collins' Company by order of
    General Macomb,
James Vandebogert, private, enlisted Dec. 19, 1812,
Peter Waldron, private, enlisted Oct. 22, 1812,
Stephen Woolman, private, enlisted Jan. 23, 1813,
John Williams, private, prisoner of war on parole,

Elisha Waterman, private, prisoner of war on parole,
Reverus Warner, private, enlisted Feb. 26, 1814,
transferred from Captain Collins' Company by
order of General Macomb,
John Warner, private, enlisted March 24, 1814, transferred from Captain Collins' Company by order of
General Macomb,
Thomas Whipple, private, enlisted Oct. 15, 1813,
transferred from Captain Collins' Company by
order of General Macomb,
Peter Winne, private, enlisted Nov. 2, 1812.

PAYROLL OF A CORPS OF LIGHT DRAGOONS, COMMANDED BY LIEUTENANT C. WRIGHT, JUNE 30, 1814.

George A. Winslow, sergeant,
Thomas P. Rogers, corporal,
Francis S. Andrews, private,
Anthony Bruce, private,
James Butler, private,
Ezekiel Billings, private,
Alexander Bell, private,
James Barnet, private,
Joseph Barron, private,
Benjamin Booth, private,
Joseph Ben, private,
Elijah Carley, private,
Hugh G. Carley, private,
Charles Flohr, private,
James Fulton, private,
Elisha Fuller, private,
Noah Hooker, private,
Ralph Hooker, private,
Edward Hammond, private,
Zimri V. Henry, private,
Eli Hurlbut, private,
Newman Hurlbut, private,

Seth Johnson, private,
John Johnson, private,
Daniel Johnson, private,
Ezra Johnson, private,
John King, private,
Thomas Lingham, private,
James Lord, private,
Mark W. Mayagen, private,
John McKinley, private,
Hiram McLaughlin, private,
William Morrow, private,
David Matthews, private,
John L. Nichols, private,
Lewis Patnor, private,
James Prout, private,
Francis Pecore, private,
Raymond Reynolds, private,
Harvey Reynolds, private,
Peter Roche, private,
Francis Rickets, private,
Reuben Rowley, private,
Moses I. Stanley, private,
Nathan Stanley, private,
Roswell B. Stanley, private,
Charles Thompson, private,
Ebenezer Trumbull, private,
Orrin Trumbull, private,
Samuel Warden, Jr., private,
Joseph Witherill, private,
Nathan Whitney, private,
Benjamin Wilds, private.

PAYROLL OF A CORPS OF ARTILLERY COMMANDED BY CAPTAIN ALEXANDER S. BROOKS, JUNE 30, 1814.

Alexander S. Brooks, captain,
Harold Smythe, first lieutenant,
Oliver Bangs, second lieutenant, enlisted June 1, 1814,
George B. Sheldon, second lieutenant, transferred to the Fourth Rifle Regiment,
Francis P. Woolsey, appointed conductor of artillery May 12, 1814,
Francis Allen, sergeant,
George Algier, sergeant, enlisted May 25, 1814,
Griffin Coles, sergeant, promoted from corporal June 1, 1814,
Francis Graves, sergeant,
Jesse W. Hollister, sergeant,
William Sharpe, sergeant,
Henry Turner, sergeant,
David H. Barker, corporal, promoted to corporal May 1, 1814,
Ebenezer Brooks, corporal,
Jacob Caldwell, corporal, promoted to corporal May 1, 1814,
James Convers, corporal,
Simeon Darling, corporal, promoted to corporal May 1, 1814,

James Hefferman, corporal,

Thomas McCammon, corporal, promoted to corporal May 1, 1814,

Jacob Winslow, corporal, reduced from sergeant June 1, 1814, to corporal, and to private June 28, 1814,

Henry Harris, musician,

John Hagerman, musician, appointed May 1, 1814,

George Layman, musician,

George Manwaring, musician, enlisted May 9, 1814,

Lyman Allen, private,

Jonathan Allen, private, discharged June 14, 1814,

William Apes, private,

Peter Anthorn, private,

Newell W. Avery, private,

Benjamin Barry, private,

William Bean, private,

Jeremiah Blake, private,

Francis Blow, private, sick in Plattsburgh hospital,

Albert Brown, private,

William Bouker, private,

Nathan Burrows, private,

William Bailey, private, enlisted May 25, 1814,

Thomas Baker, private,

John Brush, private,

Garrett Buskirk, private,

Joseph Caldwell, waiter,

James Cooper, waiter,

Andrew Clark, private,

Isaac Chapman, private,

Asa Corbin, private,

Owen Carvey, private,

Ansell Cowell, private,

George Collins, private,

Daniel H. Cary, private,
Dyson Dyer, private, enlisted June 9, 1814,
Francis Daniels, private,
Ambrose Dodd, private,
Samuel Day, private,
Aaron Durand, private,
Thomas Edmonds, private,
Joseph Emmons, private, sick in Plattsburgh hospital,
Rodolphus Fields, private,
Michael Farron, private,
John Fitzgeralds, private,
Patrick Fitzpatricks, private,
Jabez Fitch, private,
Ephriam Fox, private,
George Fisher, private, enlisted May 25, 1814,
Charles Glaspie, private, discharged and reënlisted
    May 31, 1814,
John A. Gaigar, private,
Richard Garvin, private,
John Giffin, private,
William Hunter, private,
Peter Hagerdoren, private,
Ephriam Howard, private,
Hiram Hartford, private,
Dennis Havilland, private,
Ephriam Hunt, private,
Isaac Hunt, private, died June 5, 1814,
Ephriam Howell, private, enlisted May 25, 1814,
James Irvine, private,
Dennis Kelley, private,
John B. Kelton, private,
Francis Lagg, private,
Thomas Lawrence, private,

Jacob Leonard, private,
William Lafurgy, private,
John Laughlin, private,
William McWilliams, private,
Richard McClain, private,
Edward McWaid, private,
William Mason, waiter,
Cornelius Mahan, private,
John McCale, private, enlisted May 25, 1814,
Michael McKee, private,
Duncan McGregor, private,
Mason M. Middleton, private,
John Merseveau, private,
Stewart Moore, private,
Jonathan Morrisson, private, sick in the Plattsburgh
    hospital,
Elias Mills, private, deserted June 26, 1814,
George Newton, private, discharged June 14, 1814,
Thomas Nelson, private,
Thomas Pomeroy, private, deserted June 28, 1814,
John Parker, private,
Ephriam Pray, private,
Warren Ransom, private,
Jason Richards, private, enlisted May 25, 1814,
Robert Rogers, private,
Jonathan Slaughter, private,
Thomas Stratton, private,
Samuel Sheller, private,
John Smith, private,
Shubal Short, private, sick in Plattsburgh hospital,
Peter Schmuck, private,
Peter Schampe, private,
John Shelly, private,

Peter Smith, Jr., private,
Thomas Smith, private, sick at Greenbush,
Peter Steadman, private,
Eli Stephenson, private,
William Smith, private, died June 10, 1814,
Chipman Stores, private, enlisted May 25, 1814,
David Stores, private, enlisted May 25, 1814,
William Stores, private, enlisted May 25, 1814,
Almon Stores, private, enlisted May 25, 1814,
Thomas Siddon, private,
Isaac Troinu, deserted June 29, 1814,
Chauncey Thomas, on duty at Plattsburgh ordnance,
Richard Tobin, private,
Robert Tolland, private,
Peter Van Vleck, private,
Tunis Van Pelt, private,
George Virtue, private,
Bartholomew Walsh, private,
William Warren, private, sick at Burlington,
Ephriam Whitney, private, sick at Burlington,   .
John Williams, private,
Robert Williams, private,
Hartford Willmarth, private,
George Wilson, private,
Hamilton Wilson, private, deserted June 29, 1814,
Jeremiah Woodman, private,
Peter Wilkins, private,
 Thomas Wilson, private, discharged May 22, 1814,
Michael Wells, private,
James Wormel, deserted June 24, 1814,

PAYROLL OF THE GENERAL STAFF OF THE NORTHERN ARMY, COMMANDED BY MAJOR-GENERAL GEORGE IZARD, JULY 31, 1814.

John Anderson, major of topographical engineers,
J. S. Allison, first lieutenant and aid,
John Bean, foragemaster,
Daniel Bissell, brigadier-general,
J. C. Bronaugh, hospital surgeon,
William Cummings, adjutant-general,
Sylvester Churchill, assistant inspector-general,
William Drayton, inspector-general,
M. F. Durand, barrackmaster,
Edward De Ressey, first lieutenant of engineers,
Melvin Dow, wagonmaster,
William R. Duncan, first lieutenant and brigade-major,
Robert Elliott, chaplain,
I. L. Gardner, second lieutenant and aid,
Adam Hayes, hospital surgeon,
James Hamilton, captain and aid to major-general,
Stephen Lush, Jr., judge advocate,
Joseph E. Marritt, assistant district paymaster,
Alexander Macomb, brigadier-general,
A. McIlhenny, captain and brigade-major,
M. Moore, barrackmaster,

John M. O'Connor, assistant adjutant-general,
Ninian Pinkney, inspector-general,
James Rees, deputy quartermaster-general,
Chester Root, first lieutenant and aid,
Ezra Smith, assistant deputy quartermaster-general,
Henry Stanton, second lieutenant surety,
Walter Sheldon, district paymaster,
Th. A. Smith, brigadier-general,
E. Shipp, captain and brigade-major,
Joseph G. Toppen, major of engineers,
George Trescott, second lieutenant of engineers,
Joseph Wallace, hospital surgeon's mate.

PAYROLL OF PRIVATE SERVANTS TO THE OFFICERS OF THE GENERAL STAFF, JULY 31, 1814.

Andrey, private waiter to Captain James Hamilton,
Amos Aldrich, private waiter to A. McIlhenny,
Lemuel Brown, private waiter to General Bissell,
William Crandall, private waiter to Captain E. Smith,
David, private waiter to General Alexander Macomb,
P. Ellison, private waiter to General Bissell,
Tom Van Ransalaer, private waiter to Lieutenant Allison,
Charles Truly, private waiter to General Bissell.

PAYROLL OF DISCHARGED MEN FROM A CORPS OF ARTILLERY, DRAGOONS, AND INFANTRY, AUG. 31, 1814.*

Gilbert Hankins, Knoxville, La., sergeant in Captain Hopkins' Company, Light Dragoons, discharged July 4, 1814,

Mendon Martin, Albany, N. Y., sergeant in Lieutenant Hanson's Company, Twenty-ninth Infantry, discharged July 7, 1814,

Frederick Wood, Sullivan, sergeant in Lieutenant Hanson's Company, Twenty-ninth Infantry, discharged at Cumberland Head, July 28, 1814.

Manna Hitchcock, Kingsbury, chief musician in Captain Spencer's Company, Twenty-ninth Infantry, discharged July 16, 1814,

Vanzellaer Arnold, Eaton, N. Y., private in Captain Lynds' Company, Twenty-ninth Infantry, discharged July 10, 1814,

David Bush, private in Twelfth Infantry, discharged at Champlain, August 11, 1814,

John Barker, Litchfield, private in Captain Conklin's Company, Fourth Infantry, discharged July 10, 1814,

John Blue, Shepherdstown, private in Captain Morgan's Company, Rifle Regiment, discharged August 11, 1814,

David Blaisdell, Dearfield, private in Captain Goodenoe's Company, Thirty-third Infantry, discharged August 2, 1814,

* Unless otherwise stated, these soldiers were discharged at Plattsburgh, N. Y.

Jeremiah Burley, Sanborntown, private in Captain Poland's
Company, Thirty-fourth Infantry, discharged July 5, 1814,

Moses Bumford, Northfield, private in Captain Goodenoe's
Company, Thirty-third Regiment, discharged July 5, 1814,

Asa Baker, Wiscassett, private in Captain Poland's Company,
Thirty-fourth Infantry, discharged July 6, 1814,

Nathaniel Churchill, Hubbardton, Vt., private in Captain
Wright's Company, Thirtieth Infantry, enlisted for one
year, May 15, 1813, discharged July 15, 1814, at Burlington, Vt.

Isaac Connery, Westcassett, private in Captain Binney's Company, Fourth Infantry, discharged May 28, 1814,

Thomas Connelly, Ogdensburg, private in Captain Smyth's
Company, Rifle Regiment, discharged at Champlain, July
13, 1814,

Daniel Carpenter, Jericho, Vt., private in Captain Clark's
Company, Thirtieth Infantry, discharged July 10, 1814,

Samuel Copeland, Williamsport, private in Captain Montgomery's Company, Fourteenth Infantry, discharged July 11,
1814,

Guy Carpenter, private in Captain Smythe's Company, Rifle
Regiment, discharged July 6, 1814,

John Coons, Benson, Vt., private in Captain Wright's Company,
Thirtieth Infantry, discharged July 3, 1814,

Peter Dox, Stillwater, private in Captain Lynds' Company,
Twenty-ninth Infantry, discharged July 12, 1814,

Joshua P. Downell, Portland, private in Captain Crossman's
Company, Thirty-fourth Infantry, discharged July 12, 1814,

Winthrop S. Dearborn, Candia, private in Captain Chadwick's
Company, Thirty-fourth Infantry, discharged July 5, 1814,

John Derby, Burlington, Vt., private in Captain Clark's Company, Thirtieth Infantry, discharged July 8, 1814,

Joseph De Long, Auburn, N. Y., private in Captain Spencer's

Company, Twenty-ninth Infantry, discharged July 2,
1814,
William Eaty, Shepherdstown, private in Captain Morgan's
Company, Rifle Regiment, discharged August 16, 1814,
Julian Easton, Canajohary, private in Lieutenant Hanson's
Company, Twenty-ninth Infantry, discharged July 10,
1814,
David Ellar, Rowandcock, private in Captain Nelson's Com-
pany, Tenth Infantry, discharged July 4, 1814,
Daniel Frasier, Sackett's Harbor, private in Captain Haig's
Company, Light Dragoons, discharged July 17, 1814,
James Farmer, Middlebury, private in Captain Spencer's Com-
pany, Thirteenth Infantry, discharged at Cumberland
Head, July 14, 1814,
Nathan P. Foster, Montclair, private in Captain Lynds' Com-
pany, Twenty-ninth Infantry, discharged at Chazy, August
2, 1814,
James Fisher, Leidfield, private in Captain Chadwick's Company,
Thirty-fourth Infantry, discharged April 28, 1814,
Ephraim Fox, Portland, Me., private in Captain Brooks' Com-
pany, Corps of Artillery, discharged at Cumberland Head,
July 6, 1814,
James Floyd, Boston, Mass., private in Captain Chadwick's
Company, Thirty-fourth Infantry, discharged July 3, 1814,
John Frank, Gray, Mass., private in Captain Poland's Company,
Thirty-fourth Infantry, discharged July 10, 1814,
William Green, Swanton, Vt., private in Captain Spencer's
Company, Thirtieth Infantry, discharged August 17, 1814,
John C. Garls, Baltimore, private in Captain McDonald's
Company, Fourteenth Infantry, discharged July 12, 1814,
Samuel Grosse, private in Captain Morgan's Company, Rifle
Regiment,
Hezekiah Gilbert, Hadley, N. Y., private in Captain Spencer's

Company, Twenty-ninth Infantry, discharged July 8, 1814,
Joel Hamlin, Jay, N. Y., private in Captain Spencer's Com-
pany, Twenty-ninth Infantry, discharged July 8, 1814,
Levi Hamlin, Willsboro, N. Y., private in Lieutenant Hanson's
Company, Twenty-ninth Infantry, discharged June 26,
1814,
Daniel Hawley, Berne, private in Captain Lynds' Company,
Twenty-ninth Infantry, discharged July 2, 1814,
Stephen Hersey, Sanborntown, private in Captain Poland's
Company, Thirty-fourth Infantry, discharged July 5, 1814,
Hugh Hamilton, Shepherdstown, private in Captain Morgan's
Company, Rifle Regiment, discharged at Champlain,
August 13, 1814,
Joseph Hudson, private in Captain McNeil's Company, Eleventh
Infantry,
Rowland Kellogg, Middlebury, Vt., private in Captain Vanbur-
en's Company, Twenty-ninth Infantry, discharged July 3,
1814,
James Lucas, Haverhill, N. H., private in Captain Haig's
Company of Light Dragoons, discharged July 20, 1814,
Nathan Lewis, Burlington, Vt., private in Captain Clark's
Company, Thirtieth Infantry, discharged July 7, 1814,
Arza Lee, Rutland, Vt., private in Captain Wright's Company,
Thirtieth Infantry, discharged June 15, 1814,
John Markell, Geneva, private in Captain Spencer's Company,
Twenty-ninth Infantry, discharged July 3, 1814,
Jeremiah Moore, Edgecomb, private in Captain Poland's Com-
pany, Thirty-fourth Infantry, discharged July 6, 1814,
Benjamin McCullough, Annapolis, private in Captain McIlvain's
Company, Fourteenth Infantry, discharged July 5, 1814,
Robert McKee, Harpersfield, private in Captain Spencer's
Company, Twenty-ninth Infantry, discharged July 10,
1814,

Enoch Moffitt, Hadley, N. Y., private in Captain Lynd's Company, Twenty-ninth Infantry, discharged at Cumberland Head, July 25, 1814,

James Morrisson, Philadelphia, private in Captain Young's Company, Fifteenth Infantry, discharged at Cumberland Head, August 1, 1814,

Nathaniel Marston, Dearfield, private in Captain Goodenoe's Company, Thirty-third Infantry, discharged July 25, 1814,

Iram Murry, Moreau, private in Captain Spencer's Company, Twenty-ninth Infantry, discharged June 29, 1814,

George McDonald, Standish, private in Captain Goodenoe's Company, Thirty-third Infantry, discharged at Chazy, August 12, 1814,

William McElvin, Philadelphia, private in Captain Vandalion's Company, Fifteenth Infantry, discharged at Cumberland Head, July 30, 1814,

Josiah Nichols, Middlebury, Vt., private in Captain Holley's Company, Eleventh Infantry, enlisted Feb. 20, 1813, discharged May 4, 1815,

Jacob Norton, Hadley, N. Y., private in Captain Spencer's Company, Twenty-ninth Infantry, discharged July 8, 1814,

Thaddeus Pomeroy, Schenectady, N. Y., private in Captain Leonard's Company, First Light Artillery, discharged May 28, 1814,

John Purrington, Goffstown, private in Captain Goodenoe's Company, Thirty-third Infantry, discharged July 6, 1814,

Jeremiah Passwaters, Delaware, private in Captain Gilder's Company, Fourteenth Infantry, discharged at Chazy, August 12, 1814,

Jacob Peary, Personfield, private in Eleventh Infantry, discharged at Rutland, August 13, 1814,

Silas Reynolds, Whiting, Vt., private in Captain Wright's

Company, Thirtieth Infantry, enlisted for one year, July
4, 1813, discharged July 7, 1814, at Burlington, Vt.
Francis Randolph, private in Lieutenant Butterfield's Company,
Fourth Infantry, discharged June 27, 1814,
David Richardson, Edgecomb, private in Captain Chadwick's
Company, Thirty-fourth Infantry, discharged July 5, 1814,
Ebenezer Russell, Salmontown, private in Captain Poland's
Company, Thirty-fourth Infantry, discharged July 11, 1814,
Jonathan Rose, Westchester, private in Captain McIlvain's
Company, Fourteenth Infantry, discharged July 5, 1814,
Nathaniel Rose, Lancaster, private in Captain McIlvain's
Company, Fourteenth Infantry, discharged August 6, 1814,
Nathan Stiles, Bridgetown, Maine, private in Captain Branch's
Company, Light Artillery, discharged at Champlain, July 1,
1814,
Ira Sevey, Meredith, private in Captain Poland's Company,
Thirty-fourth Infantry, discharged July 10, 1814,
Isaac Stewart, Bridport, Vt., private in Captain Spencer's Com-
pany, Thirtieth Infantry, discharged July 11, 1814,
Bastian I. Stiples, Berne, private in Captain Lynds' Company,
Twenty-ninth Infantry, discharged July 1, 1814,
Willard Sanborn, Sanborntown, private in Captain Chadwick's
Company, Thirty-fourth Infantry, discharged July 11,
1814,
Luther Stiles, Bridgetown, Maine, private in Captain Branch's
Company, Light Artillery, discharged at Champlain, June
29, 1814,
John H. Talbott, Annapolis, private in Captain McIlvain's
Company, Fourteenth Infantry, discharged August 16, 1814,
William Thomas, Philadelphia, private in Captain Young's
Company, Fifteenth Infantry, discharged August 1, 1814,
John S. Workman, private in Captain Vanburen's Company,
Twenty-ninth Infantry, discharged June 8, 1814,

Ephraim Willey, Alexandria, private in Captain Montgomery's
    Company, Fourteenth Infantry, discharged June 24, 1814,
David Willmarth, Eaton, N. Y., private in Captain Lynds'
    Company, Twenty-ninth Infantry, discharged July 8, 1814,
John Wilkinson, private in Captain Smythe's Company, Rifle
    Regiment, discharged July 6, 1814,
George Wilkins, Ovid, N. Y., private in Lieutenant Hanson's
    Company, Twenty-ninth Infantry, discharged July 8, 1814,
Silas Waterman, St. Albans, Vt., private in Captain Sanford's
    Company, Thirtieth Infantry, discharged at Burlington,
    Vt., May 31, 1814.

PAYROLL OF A CORPS OF ARTILLERY, DRAGOONS, AND INFANTRY, TO SEPT. 30, 1814.

John Waterhouse, sergeant-major,
Abraham C. Fowler, sergeant,
Israel W. Frisbee, corporal,
Noah Sinclear, corporal,
John Penn, musician,
Timothy Sullivan, artificer,
Abraham Derby, corps artificer,
William Albrough, private,
Dan Allen, private,
Meshack W. Blake, private,
Joshua Bishop, private,
Offin Barrett, private,
Jacob Chase, private,
Timothy Collins, private, .
Thaddeus Curtis, private,
Josiah Davis, private,
Henry Diamond, private,
John Drout, private,
William Edwards, private,
Thomas Eades, private,
John Edwards, private,
Rice Edwards, private,
Frederick Fife, private,

Samuel Grosse, private,
Robert Gotham, private,
Reuben Hodging, private,
Samuel Haviland, private,
William House, private,
Thomas Ingersoll, private,
James Jones, private,
George T. Magee, private,
Christopher Martin, private,
John Prosser, private,
James Parliment, private,
Daniel Pierce, private,
Jonathan Rich, private,
James Reynolds, private,
Andrew Salisbury, private,
Moses S. Small, private,
Thomas Sepiom, private,
Nathan Starkey, private,
Edwin F. Stoddard, private,
Levi Stewart, private,
Matthew B. Stephens, private,
Isaac Tucker, private,
Joseph Tucker, private,
Asa Thornton, private,
William Wade, private,
Jacob Wills, private,
John Whitaker, private.

FROM A PAYROLL ENTITLED "PAYROLL OF
DISCHARGED MEN TO DEC. 31, 1815. FOR
ARREARAGES OF MONTHLY WAGES, AD-
DITIONAL PAY, RETAINED BOUNTY,
AND PAY AND SUBSISTENCE FOR
TRAVELLING HOME."*

CAPTAIN SANFORD'S COMPANY, THIRTIETH INFANTRY, DIS-
CHARGED JUNE 17, 1815, AT BURLINGTON, VT.

Derrick Brown, sergeant, Pownal, Vt., enlisted April 27, 1814,
John W. Drewry, sergeant, Holden, Mass., enlisted July 11, 1814,
Chauncey Johnson, sergeant, Middlebury, Vt., enlisted March
    17, 1814,
John W. Robinson, sergeant, Manchester, Vt., enlisted Feb. 24,
    1814,
Nathaniel Sanford, sergeant, Sandgate, Vt., enlisted Feb. 25,
    1814,
William T. Starks, sergeant, Pownal, Vt., enlisted Feb. 18,
    1814,
Daniel Stewart, corporal, Bristol, Mass., enlisted March 18, 1814,
Samuel Slocum, corporal, Schaticoke, N. Y., enlisted Feb. 24,
    1814,
Reuben Tousley, corporal, Dorset, Vt., enlisted Feb. 13, 1814,
Nathaniel Wood, corporal, Whitehall, N. Y., enlisted March
    2, 1814,

*Unless otherwise stated, the enlistment was for during the war.

Lyman Lewis, fifer, Wethersfield, Vt., enlisted Feb. 25, 1814,
John Alfred, private, Sheldon, Vt., enlisted March 24, 1814,
William Adcock, private, Burlington, Vt., enlisted March 12,
    1814,
Barzilla Bradford, private, Tunbridge, Vt., enlisted May 27,
    1814,
Jacob Brown, private, Wolfsborough, enlisted March 28, 1814,
John Baldwin, private, Newark, enlisted April 1, 1814,
Friend Beaman, private, Bridport, Vt., enlisted April 2, 1814,
Thomas Bentley, private, St. Albans, Vt., enlisted May 7, 1814,
Joseph Carter, private, Groton, Vt., enlisted April 9, 1814,
George Campbell, private, Middletown, Vt., enlisted April 23,
    1814,
Chester Cunnell, private, Warren, Conn., enlisted August 9,
    1814,
Stephen C. Cobb, private, Schaticoke, N. Y., enlisted March
    24, 1814,
Joseph Campbell, private, Benson, Vt., enlisted Feb. 10, 1814,
Samuel Carter, private, Groton, Vt., enlisted April 9, 1814,
Paul I. Cheney, private, Waterford, Vt., enlisted July 25, 1814,
Joseph P. Clark, private, Swanton, Vt., enlisted Feb. 24, 1814,
William A. Cheney, private, Pownal, Vt., enlisted March 24,
    1814,
Asa W. Durkee, private, Pittsford, Vt., enlisted March 10, 1814,
John P. Dalton, private, Lemingston, enlisted Dec. 22, 1813,
George W. Dunton, private, Burlington, Vt., enlisted Feb. 27,
    1814,
Zephaniah Ellis, private, New Haven, Vt., enlisted Dec. 30,
    1813,
Cornwall Fenton, private, Wells, Vt., enlisted Feb. 28, 1814,
Salmon Frank, private, Troy, N. Y., enlisted Sept. 25, 1813,
Elijah H. Fields, private, Northfield, Vt., enlisted August 17,
    1814,

James Goodyear, private, Cornwall, Vt., enlisted Dec. 22, 1813,
William Gage, private, Dorset, Vt., enlisted July 2, 1814,
Joseph U. Green, private, Hanover, N. H., enlisted March 17,
1814,
John Hooker, private, Ferrisburgh, Vt., enlisted April 23, 1814,
Joseph W. Hibbard, private, Charlton, enlisted Feb. 5, 1814,
Thomas Hale, private, Poultney, Vt., enlisted March 13, 1814,
John O. Joy, private, Plattsburgh, N. Y., enlisted Dec. 23, 1813,
William Jackson, private, enlisted June 18, 1814,
Philip Kineston, private, Milton, Vt., enlisted April 2, 1814,
Medad Kellogg, private, Cavendish, Vt., enlisted Feb. 27, 1814,
Marshall Lee, private, Pawlet, Vt., enlisted Feb. 26, 1814,
Isaac Learned, private, Fairfax, Vt., enlisted April 28, 1814,
Mark W. Mazazem, private, Cornwall, Vt., enlisted April 11,
1814,
Elihu Miller, private, Whitehall, N. Y., enlisted Feb. 12, 1814,
Thomas Merritt, private, Cornwall, Vt., enlisted March 17,
1814,
Samuel Osgood, private, Boston, Mass., enlisted March 15,
1814,
Anthony Phillips, private, enlisted for one year, May 12, 1813,
Nathaniel Prouty, private, Middlebury, Vt., enlisted April 21,
1814,
Jonathan Parker, private, Clarendon, Vt., enlisted Feb. 26,
1814,
Hiram W. Rockwell, private, Cornwall, Vt., enlisted April 25,
1814,
Thomas Simmons, private, Cheshire, Mass., enlisted Feb. 15,
1814,
Obed Sheldon, private, St. Albans, Vt., enlisted Feb. 16, 1814,
Loyd Santer, private, Panton, Vt., enlisted March 20, 1814,
Martin Smith, private, Arlington, Vt., enlisted Feb. 14, 1814,
Ethan Spencer, private, Williston, Vt., enlisted Feb. 13, 1814,

Samuel L. Stevens, private, Epping, N. H., enlisted June 17, 1814,

Luther Stockwell, private, Shaftsbury, Vt., enlisted Feb. 24, 1814,

James Thomas, private, Boston, Mass., enlisted June 13, 1814,

Samuel Tyler, private, enlisted Feb. 23, 1814,

Whittlesey Wright, private, Bristol, Vt., enlisted March 27, 1814,

Jesse White, private, Pownal, Vt., enlisted May 25, 1814,

John H. Wise, private, Providence, R. I., enlisted March 29, 1814,

Jeremiah Williams, private, Providence, R. I., enlisted May 11, 1814.

CAPTAIN TAYLOR'S COMPANY, THIRTIETH INFANTRY, DIS-
CHARGED JUNE 20, 1815, AT BURLINGTON, VT.

Silas Bevenstock, sergeant, Shrewsbury, Vt., enlisted May 16, 1814,

Thomas Conelly, sergeant, Plattsburgh, N. Y., enlisted August 10, 1814,

Patrick Downey, sergeant, Sandy Hill, N. Y., enlisted Oct. 11, 1814,

John Poter, sergeant, Lanesborough, Mass., enlisted July 26, 1814,

Joseph Prescott, sergeant, Montpelier, Vt., enlisted April 12, 1814,

Nathan Smith, sergeant, Shrewsbury, Vt., enlisted May 16, 1814,

Elijah C. Wingate, sergeant, Buxton, Mass., enlisted Oct. 6, 1814,

John Wright, sergeant, Pownal, Vt., enlisted March 24, 1814,

James C. Angel, corporal, Pownal, Vt., enlisted May 7, 1814,

Peter Brown, corporal, enlisted Sept. 28, 1814,
Daniel Drake, corporal, Clarendon, Vt., enlisted Jan. 16, 1815,
Ebenezer Farnum, corporal, Pownal, Vt., enlisted April 16, 1814,
William S. Hale, corporal, Pittsford, Vt., enlisted June 20, 1814,
John Ladd, corporal, Lansingburgh, N. Y., enlisted Oct. 2, 1814,
Daniel Sisson, corporal, Berne, N. Y., enlisted August 5, 1814,
Thomas O'Connor, drummer, enlisted Dec. 24, 1814,
Harry Bottles, private, Berne, N. Y., enlisted Sept. 11, 1814,
Daniel Bemis, private, Pittsford, Vt., enlisted August 5, 1814,
William Bolles, private, Berne, N. Y., enlisted Sept. 14, 1814,
Nathaniel Buel, private, Lansingburgh, N. Y., enlisted Oct. 8, 1814,
John Churchill, private, Berne, N. Y., enlisted Sept. 10, 1814,
Alexander N. Cotter, private, Benson, Vt., enlisted April 22, 1814,
John Dunn, private, Sandy Hill, N. Y., enlisted Sept. 24, 1814,
Abraham Doty, private, Schoharie, N. Y., enlisted Sept. 18, 1814,
David Durkee, private, Pittsford, Vt., enlisted June 20, 1814,
Jabez Dexter, private, Washington, N. H., enlisted July 14, 1814,
Charles Doughty, private, Sandy Hill, N. Y., enlisted Oct. 22, 1814,
John Daniels, private, Utica, N. Y., enlisted Oct. 6, 1814,
Abiatha Evans, private, Schoharie, N. Y., enlisted Sept. 18, 1814,
Cyrus K. Francis, private, Pownal, Vt., enlisted Sept. 19, 1814,
Benjamin B. Goodrich, private, Pittsford, Vt., enlisted June 20, 1814,
John N. Harris, private, Lansingburgh, N. Y., enlisted Oct. 3, 1814,

Walter Houghton, private, Pittsford, Vt., enlisted June 20, 1814,
Simeon Hammond, private, Westminster, Vt., enlisted July 29,
   1814,
Timothy Herrington, private, Ticonderoga, N. Y., enlisted Oct.
   31, 1814,
Asa Jackson, private, Rutland, Vt., enlisted June 24, 1814,
Graten Jackson, private, Rutland, Vt., enlisted June 24, 1814,
David Johnson, private, Fairfax, Vt., enlisted Jan. 5, 1815,
William Jordan, private, Woodstock, Vt., enlisted May 22,1814,
William Kelley, private, Sandy Hill, N. Y., enlisted Oct. 25,
   1814,
Ephraim Leonard, private, Lansingburgh, N. Y., enlisted
   Oct. 4, 1814,
Frederick Laughlin, private, Georgia, Vt., enlisted Oct. 11, 1814,
William Laiton, private, Schoharie, N. Y., enlisted Sept. 10,
   1814,
David McCoy, private, Dorset, Vt., enlisted July 14, 1814,
Isaac Mosher, private, Lansingburgh, N. Y., enlisted Oct. 10,
   1814,
Jacob Noys, private, Poultney, Vt., enlisted April 14, 1814,
John O. Neal, private, Sandy Hill, N. Y., enlisted Dec. 13,
   1814,
Ephraim Owens, private, Pittsford, Vt., enlisted June 29, 1814,
Michael Owens, private, Sandy Hill, N. Y., enlisted Oct. 14,
   1814,
David Putnam, private, Vergennes, Vt., enlisted Dec. 20, 1814,
Samuel Plant, private, Sandy Hill, N. Y., enlisted Oct. 28, 1814,
Silas Remington, private, Rupert, Vt., enlisted June 15, 1814,
Alvin Rouse, private, Sandy Hill, N. Y., enlisted Dec. 1, 1814,
William Stockwell, private, Williamstown, Vt., enlisted Dec. 5,
   1814,
Elijah W. Sawyer, private, Montpelier, Vt., enlisted June 17,
   1814,

Timothy Skinner, private, Montpelier, Vt., enlisted Sept. 17, 1814,

Lemuel Smeadley, private, Williamstown, Mass., enlisted June 24, 1814,

Hiram Tompson, private, Lansingburgh, N. Y., enlisted Oct. 30, 1814,

Squire Wood, private, Danby, Vt., enlisted April 12, 1814,

Benjamin Whitman, private, Middletown, Vt., enlisted May 17, 1814,

John Williams, private, Springtown, enlisted Nov. 16, 1814,

William Wisgawen, private, Berne, N. Y., enlisted July 30, 1814,

Peter Winney, private, Northumberland, N. Y., enlisted Dec. 7, 1814,

Jacob Wisgawen, private, Berne, N. Y., enlisted August 4, 1814.

www.ingramcontent.com/pod-product-compliance
Lightning Source LLC
Chambersburg PA
CBHW061741270326
41928CB00011B/2328